"What a lovely little book! I have a few books like this in my library that I return to often, so it is a delight to add to that collection this gentle encouragement to have a refreshing life, or maybe a life that is constantly being refreshed. Ajith Fernando will encourage you with his wisdom, from a lifetime on the front lines. I'm thankful for this gift to weary Christians."

Paul E. Miller, author, *A Praying Life*; *J-Curve*; and *A Praying Church*

"*Joyful Perseverance* is a gift that beautifully arises out of Ajith Fernando's reflections on over forty years of Christian ministry. As it turns out, our ministries are not sustained by career advancements, titles, or platform opportunities. Rather, we persevere through union with Christ who grants us the deeper gifts of grace and gratitude in the midst of times of sorrow and lament. This book is a treasure for those who long for a ministry that is punctuated not by burnout and despair but instead by joyful perseverance in the presence of Christ."

Timothy C. Tennent, President and Professor of World Christianity, Asbury Theological Seminary

"In *Joyful Perseverance*, Ajith Fernando describes what it means to live out the gospel in demanding times and dangerous places. This is a huge gift to us all. For over four decades, Fernando and I have journeyed together in ministry, which has given me the opportunity to know that what you read in this remarkable text has been tested. Fernando has been relentless in finding life and inspiration in the God he loves and serves. Now we in our own moments of trials and wanderings can join with him in discovering those sources of joy which give life to carry on."

Brian C. Stiller, global ambassador, The World Evangelical Alliance

"My pastor once told me to choose a book by its author, and that advice has proved to be wise counsel. Ajith Fernando is someone I want to learn from, and in *Joyful Perseverance*, the allure of the subject combines with the authenticity of the author to make this book irresistible."

Colin S. Smith, Senior Pastor, The Orchard, Arlington Heights, Illinois; Founder and Bible Teacher, Open the Bible

"Finishing well is perhaps the greatest desire, and the greatest challenge, in the life of any Christian leader. In *Joyful Perseverance*, Ajith Fernando distills over forty years of leadership experience to produce a volume of extraordinary biblical insight and practical wisdom for finishing well. Having known Fernando for over four decades as my mentor and friend, I'm thrilled that countless others can now benefit from the wisdom of a remarkable leader, whose authenticity and consistency some of us have been privileged to see up close and personally."

Ivor Poobalan, Principal, Colombo Theological Seminary; Cochair, Theology Working Group, Lausanne Movement

"I love Ajith Fernando! His example of over forty years of joyful, sacrificial perseverance inspires me. God has enabled him to document his own experience of God's grace in a way that invites readers to experience that grace afresh and to let it heal our wounds. Fernando, enabled by the Holy Spirit, sees the pastoral dimension of biblical texts that both diagnose and treat the perils that keep us from abiding in God's grace. In addition to scriptural insights and candid recollections of his own shortcomings, Fernando, ever the reader, fills his pages with maxims and nuggets from the faithful, adding his own hard-won insights. With many words of wisdom, Fernando skillfully plies his trade as a physician of the soul and draws us back to our gracious God. Read it and rejoice; let the living Lord, our triune God, enable you to persevere."

Greg R. Scharf, Professor Emeritus of Homiletics and Pastoral Theology, Trinity Evangelical Divinity School

"Ajith Fernando is a remarkably gifted pastor and teacher, with considerable charisma. But what I love most in him is his deep and holy commitment to honor God. This book offers a window into his heart."

Tim Stafford, author

Joyful Perseverance

Joyful Perseverance

Staying Fresh through the Ups and Downs of Ministry

Ajith Fernando

Foreword by Thomas R. Schreiner

CROSSWAY®

WHEATON, ILLINOIS

Joyful Perseverance: Staying Fresh through the Ups and Downs of Ministry

© 2024 by Ajith Fernando

Published by Crossway
　　　1300 Crescent Street
　　　Wheaton, Illinois 60187

Published in association with the literary agency of Wolgemuth & Wilson.

Royalties from the sale of this book will go for literature and education projects in Sri Lanka.

Cover design: Jordan Singer

First printing 2024

Printed in the United States of America

Trade paperback ISBN: 978-1-4335-9376-5
ePub ISBN: 978-1-4335-9378-9
PDF ISBN: 978-1-4335-9377-2

Library of Congress Cataloging-in-Publication Data

Names: Fernando, Ajith, author.
Title: Joyful perseverance : staying fresh through the ups and downs of ministry / Ajith Fernando ; foreword by Thomas R. Schreiner.
Description: Wheaton, Illinois : Crossway, 2024. | Includes bibliographical references and index. | Summary: "Explores how one can remain fresh with joy in Christian ministry over the long haul"— Provided by publisher.
Identifiers: LCCN 2023053500 (print) | LCCN 2023053501 (ebook) | ISBN 9781433593765 (trade paperback) | ISBN 9781433593789 (epub) | ISBN 9781433593772 (pdf)
Subjects: LCSH: Church work. | Joy | Perseverance (Ethics)
Classification: LCC BV4400 .F47 2024 (print) | LCC BV4400 (ebook) | DDC 253—dc23/eng/20240222
LC record available at https://lccn.loc.gov/2023053500
LC ebook record available at https://lccn.loc.gov/2023053501

Crossway is a publishing ministry of Good News Publishers.

VP			33	32	31	30	29	28	27	26	25	24
15	14	13	12	11	10	9	8	7	6	5	4	3	2	1

To
Albert and Catherine Lee
Chiu Yau and Wingyan Mok
Edward and June Lee
Bishop Kim Seng and Ai Mai Kuan
Lawrence and Agnes James
Michael and Connie Cheong
Representing a host of East Asian Christians
who have blessed me by their friendship

Contents

Foreword

SOMETIMES WHEN I read a book, I wish everyone would read it. That conviction seized me repeatedly as I read this powerful and prophetic book by Ajith Fernando. I have read Fernando's books for many years, and spiritual insight and, dare I say, freshness have been characteristic of his work. What underlies this book is Scripture, which is hardly surprising since the Bible contains the words of life—the words that, by God's Spirit, transform us and make us glad. We need to be filled with the Spirit (Eph. 5:18), but we will be filled with the Spirit only if we are also filled with the word (Col. 3:16). Fernando reminds us that if God's word isn't residing in our minds and hearts, then there will be no spiritual power, no enduement from on high. God uses the ordinary means of grace to sustain us on our journey to the heavenly city.

Another mark of this book is authenticity. We sense and know as we read that Ajith Fernando isn't spinning a tale. He has been in ministry for forty-seven years, and he confesses his own weaknesses and struggles. He tells the story of all of us as we struggle with insecurity, weakness, pride, lust, bitterness, resentment, overwork, and underwork. Yes, the treasure of the gospel is indeed in earthen vessels (2 Cor. 4:7). Paul acknowledges that as believers we suffer affliction, are plagued by doubts, and suffer from attacks by others (2 Cor. 4:8–9). Sometimes, as Fernando points out, those attacks even come from other Christians, sometimes even from our friends. You won't find here a simplistic guide for how to have a happy life and how to overcome all your problems. Life isn't easy, and that message is communicated realistically.

At the same time, we are not left merely with the message that life is hard. We all know that! Or if you don't know it now, you will know it soon enough. Even though we experience sorrow, we are also full of joy in the midst of sorrow (2 Cor. 6:10). Fernando reminds us that we know God—what an amazing gift!—in the Father, the Son, and the Holy Spirit. God's love is available to strengthen and sustain us throughout our lives. Because God loves us, we don't have to hide our weaknesses, insecurities, or sins from him (or from others). In the midst of our weaknesses he gives us strength. Indeed, the joy of the Lord is our strength even in the hardest times in our lives (Neh. 8:10). When we think we can't forgive that person who has hurt us so badly, the person who fills us with resentment, God gives us power to love and to forgive. Still, we may struggle with the same issue tomorrow, and once again we will need God's grace to fill us afresh.

One other theme that stands out is the emphasis on friendship, on colleagues in ministry. We have a great God, but God has also given us brothers and sisters, the corporate body, the church. We need regular fellowship with other believers and to be involved vitally in the church of Jesus Christ. When we are hurt, we can be tempted to withdraw from gathering regularly with other believers. In the church the Lord gives us friends, and he comforts us not only by his own presence but also with others who love us.

Read this book. Meditate on its message. Pray as you read it. It inspired me afresh to forget the things that are past and to live for the glory of God and to run the race to the end (Phil. 3:12–14).

Thomas R. Schreiner

Introduction

MY THIRTIETH ANNIVERSARY of ministry with Youth for Christ, Sri Lanka, fell on July 15, 2006, while I was traveling in the United States. I did not have any preaching appointments that day. I was staying at the home of my friends, Pastor David and Karin Livingston, in Minneapolis. Their home was close to the Mississippi River, and I decided to walk to the river and spend the morning on its bank with my little New Testament, my notebook, and the Lord. I began to read from the beginning of 2 Corinthians, and I got stuck at chapter 4. It starts with the affirmation that we do not lose heart, because our ministry is by the mercy of God. Reflecting on this led me to prepare a series of talks on "Secrets of Long-Term Freshness in Ministry." With time, I thought I must write a book on this topic, but I thought it would be best to do so after a few more years in vocational ministry. Now after forty-seven years I believe that time has come.

Since stepping down in 2011 after thirty-five years as leader of Youth for Christ, Sri Lanka, I have remained on Youth for Christ staff. My main ministry has been mentoring and counseling Youth for Christ staff and pastors, as well as younger leaders from other Christian groups and churches. Over time, I have grown in the conviction that the key to longevity in ministry is constantly experiencing God's grace and letting grace heal the wounds that come from disappointments and challenges in life and ministry. So this book is mainly about applying grace to our lives and ministries, and avoiding those things that hinder grace. The topics I have chosen to discuss are first the result of much biblical reflection, but also the result of observing recurring patterns of positive and negative effects that certain experiences, lifestyles, attitudes, and decisions have on Christian leaders, including me. Over the years I have tried to reflect and teach about how the Bible addresses those issues.

This book is not a comprehensive guide to freshness. I have tried to keep the book relatively small and have not addressed some important issues, some of which others are more qualified to speak on, including the following:

- The need for rest and a regular Sabbath (I briefly address this in chap. 3).
- The need for recreation, exercise, and times to enjoy the beauty of creation.
- The need for hobbies that bring relaxation.
- The need to have fun times, especially with family and friends.[1]
- The need to have relaxed times with family in conversation, in prayer, and around God's word.[2]
- The need to confront issues that affect one's emotional and spiritual health and possibly get some help with those issues.

---

1 I am grateful to my fitness and life coach son-in-law Rabindranath Refuge for alerting me to the first four points.
2 This fifth point comes from my wife.

- The need for ministry to individuals, such as personal witness and discipling, which helps keep us on our toes spiritually. I have written a whole book on discipling.[3]

I believe that after all these years, I am still excited about ministry. I know I have made big mistakes, and often have failed to live up to the high standards of my calling. I am often overwhelmed by all the weaknesses I struggle with. But I can honestly say with Paul that, "having this ministry by the mercy of God, [I] do not lose heart" (2 Cor. 4:1). Praise God! His grace is sufficient to sustain and use even the weakest of his servants.

Toward the end of this book, I will show how grace is often mediated to our lives through the body of Christ. I must acknowledge the way God has blessed me through the communities to which I belong. I have been a member of the Youth for Christ family for almost sixty years, for ten years as a volunteer and then as a staff worker. It is in this context that I learned the secrets of effective ministry. I have been particularly blessed through two accountability groups from the Youth for Christ family to which I belong. Most of the material in this book was taught to the staff of Youth for Christ. This book has been greatly enriched by their lively and frank responses to what I taught.

Then there is the Nugegoda Methodist Church, of which my wife and I have been members for more than forty years and where I now do most of my grassroots ministry. I'm grateful, too, for my biological family. I was blessed to be born into a loving Christian home, and I always thank God for my parents, B. E. and Malini Fernando, and my four siblings: Kumar, Duleep, Priyan,

---

3   Ajith Fernando, *Discipling in a Multicultural World* (Wheaton, IL: Crossway, 2019).

and Anusha. My wife, Nelun, has been the greatest human medium of grace in my life. My two children, Nirmali and Asiri, their spouses Refuge and Cheryl, and our four grandchildren, Avisha, Sanil, Yasas, and Yeheli, cause my wife and me to abound with joy.

I am very happy to be working with Crossway once again, and I am grateful to be able to benefit from the expert editing skills of Tara Davis. I am amazed by how much I have been blessed by the body of Christ!

I have written many books about Christian life and ministry, so it is inevitable that some points in those books have made their way into this book also (though I hardly consulted those books when writing this one). This is especially true of my book *The Call to Joy and Pain*.[4] Hopefully the points are presented here with a freshness that has come out of many more years of experience since writing my earlier books.

My hope is that this book would help readers to develop resources to help them continue to persevere joyfully over the long haul in the service to which God has called them.

---

4 Ajith Fernando, *The Call to Joy and Pain: Embracing Suffering in Your Ministry* (Wheaton, IL: Crossway, 2007).

1

What Do We Mean by Freshness?

THIS BOOK IS ABOUT maintaining freshness in ministry over the long haul. Freshness is a difficult concept to define; it can mean different things according to the context one is describing. So I will begin by explaining what I mean by freshness in this book, first by listing what it is *not* and then by explaining what it *is*.

What Freshness Does Not Mean

First, when we talk of freshness in ministry, we do not mean *maintaining good physical health while we minister*. Many great servants of God struggled with poor health. One of the most influential seventeenth-century Christian leaders and authors, Richard Baxter (1615–1691), struggled with ill health most of his life. He did not have good experiences with the medical personnel who attended to him.[1] He seemed to live with the sense that he was going through "the valley of the shadow of death." He is credited with the statement,

---

1   See Tim Cooper, "Richard Baxter and His Physicians," *Social History of Medicine*, 20, no. 1 (April 2007): 1–19. You can access a summary of this article at https://academic.oup.com /shm/article-abstract/20/1/1/2332129?redirectedFrom=PDF.

"I preached as never sure to preach again, and as a dying man to dying men."[2] Baxter wrote the classic book on ministry *The Reformed Pastor*, of which Amazon lists nine different editions in print today. He continued to preach until he died at the age of seventy-six.

Second, we do not mean *having a motivated, enthusiastic approach* to the tasks we perform. Many great actors, politicians, scientists, and businessmen showed exemplary enthusiasm to the end of their lives, but they did not follow Christ.

Third, when we speak of freshness, we do not mean *having a bubbly personality* that always exudes joy. The great leaders Martin Luther (1483–1546) and Charles Spurgeon (1834–1892) often struggled with bouts of depression, but they ministered with power to the end of their lives.

Fourth, we do not mean a life of *climbing the ecclesiastical ladder*. There is a wrong idea that one's position in an organization or church is a measure of his or her fruitfulness in service. We have books proclaiming that everyone can be a leader if they just follow the right formula. But Christian fruitfulness is not defined by position in the church. This kind of false teaching has left many unnecessarily feeling that they are unsuccessful in their service for God or that they have been deprived of positions they deserve. The Bible and church history show that those who are not leaders by that definition can be great and exemplary servants of God. If one were to define a leader as "someone who has followers," then all Christians can be leaders.[3] All Christians can influence people to follow God's paths. But not all great Christians will rise to high positions on the ecclesiastical ladder.

2 "Richard Baxter: Moderate in an Age of Extremes," *Christianity Today*, https://www .christianitytoday.com. Accessed June 25, 2022.

3 Peter Drucker, *Managing for the Future* (New York: Routledge, 2011), 103.

Brother Lawrence (1614–1691) served in a monastery kitchen for thirty years. At first, he resented having to do such work, but a vital experience with God made him realize that everything he did, even washing dishes, was done for God. He lived to a ripe old age and left some letters and spiritual notes which were compiled after his death under the title *The Practice of the Presence of God.* That little book became one of the most influential spiritual classics in the history of the church. Many people talk about the value of servant leadership these days. But few are willing to embrace a lifestyle of real servanthood, because that does not fit in with their understanding of what it means to be successful.

What Freshness Means

Let's now look at what we mean by freshness in ministry. My basic affirmation is that it is a life that continues to minister in the Spirit. Let me unpack that. First, we are talking about a life where the grace of God is evident through God's constant presence, equipping, and leading. Paul saw all his ministry as coming from the mercy of God (2 Cor. 4:1). This means that what is most important is not our service—what we do for God—but grace—what God does for us. As we shall see, excellence in ministry is important to us because we do it for the honor of a glorious God. *But our primary aim in life is the pursuit of God.* More than anything else, we want to guard our relationship with him with a sense of urgency, and deal with anything that hinders that relationship. Even when things seem to be going wrong and God seems to be far away, our primary desire is God. As the psalmist said in a dark time of his life,

As a deer pants for flowing streams,
    so pants my soul for you, O God.

My soul thirsts for God,
> for the living God. (Ps. 42:1–2)

The primary source of freshness in our lives is not our vocational fulfillment through using our gifts, though that is important. It is not our adventures in ministry as we try new and creative things, though those are also important. It is *our love relationship with God.* It is the thrill of being on speaking terms with the King of kings and of receiving his blessing.

Second, people experiencing freshness surely have had many painful, sorrowful, and disappointing experiences in life. But while they may live with sorrow over them, *negative feelings and bitterness about those experiences do not constantly influence their moods and their interactions* with people. They have been comforted by God. Before recounting a painful experience, Paul said, "Blessed be the God and Father of our Lord Jesus Christ, the Father of mercies and God of all comfort, who comforts us in all our affliction, so that we may be able to comfort those who are in any affliction, with the comfort with which we ourselves are comforted by God" (2 Cor. 1:3–4). He had overcome bitterness through God's comfort.

Third, people maintaining freshness have *hearts that are receptive to letting God's love* flow into and out of their lives. Paul said, "God's love has been poured into our hearts through the Holy Spirit" (Rom. 5:5). The word *poured* has the idea of "flooding" (PHILLIPS). The experience of love also combats feelings of bitterness. The flood of God's love challenges the dominance of bitterness and sweeps it away. That love "compels" them to let love flow out of their lives in service (2 Cor. 5:14 NIV). Ministry is an overflow of experiencing God's love. My friend Susan Pearlman, a leader in

Jews for Jesus, once said, "Burnout takes place when the wick and not the oil is burning." If we tap into the oil of God's inexhaustible supply of love, that love will keep energizing our service. And our lives will be kept bright with the joy of experiencing love.

Fourth, freshness in ministry is characterized by *thankfulness for the privilege of being God's servant*. After describing the painful experience to which we alluded above, Paul said, "But thanks be to God, who in Christ *always* leads us in triumphal procession, and through us spreads the fragrance of the knowledge of him *everywhere*" (2 Cor. 2:14). "Always" and "everywhere" we find cause for thanksgiving, even after painful experiences. Paul looked at life and ministry not through the lens of problems but with a heart full of thanksgiving for being God's servant.

Fifth, people experiencing freshness are *passionate about ministry to the end*. Again we turn to Paul. He said, "Never be lacking in zeal, but keep your spiritual fervor, serving the Lord" (Rom. 12:11 NIV). When in his late eighties, John Wesley wrote in his diary, "My eyes are now waxed dim; my natural force is abated. However, while I can, I would fain do a little for God before I drop into the dust."[4] The passion for ministry was still there!

Years ago I heard a story of an elderly Christian who was close to death. A doctor examined him and, when leaving the room, whispered something to his attendant. The patient asked the attendant what the doctor had said. The attendant answered that he had told him that he had only a few moments to live. The old saint promptly said, "Then quick, get me on my knees and let me spend the few moments I have praying for the salvation of the world." Even when facing death, he had not lost his freshness.

4 Albert C. Outler, ed., *The Works of John Wesley* (Grand Rapids, MI: Baker, 1987), 4:483.

Further Reflection

What unavoidable aspects of your personality or circumstances seem to threaten your freshness? How will you maintain freshness while living with these features?

2

It Is All of Grace

DR. J. ROBERT CLINTON conducted a now-famous study of how leaders in the Old and New Testaments finished their tenures as leaders. Of those about whom he was able to get sufficient data, Clinton determined that about one in three finished well. Commenting on the contemporary scene, he said, "Anecdotal evidence from today indicates that this ratio is probably generous. Probably less than 1 in 3 are finishing well today."[1] *It does not have to be so!*

The Promise of Longevity

The Bible promises that God is able to keep us faithful and fruitful to the end. What Paul said to the Philippians can be applied to all servants of Christ: "And I am sure of this, that he who began a good work in you will bring it to completion at the day of Jesus Christ" (Phil. 1:6). Paul said of himself, "I know whom I have believed, and I am convinced that he is able to guard until that day what has been entrusted to me" (2 Tim. 1:12). In both of these verses, the

---

1 J. Robert Clinton, "Finishing Well—Six Characteristics," 2007, http://storage.cloversites.com /missouristateassociationoffreewillbaptists/documents/Finishing-Well-Six-Characteristics.pdf.

primary reason we can finish well is not because we possess some great skill. It is because God is able to protect us.

We do not just survive in ministry. We can serve God with joy and zeal until the end. Paul told the Romans: "Never flag in zeal, be aglow with the Spirit, serve the Lord" (Rom. 12:11 RSV). In this book we hope to look at ways in which the glow of the Spirit can continue as we serve the Lord until the end of our lives.

Over the years it has been my sad lot to meet and counsel with many servants of God who have lost this glow. My own effort to maintain the glow, my reading of the Scriptures, and the opportunity to counsel and mentor many leaders have led me to the conclusion that disappointments along the way, wrong attitudes relating to ourselves and our experiences, and the failure to avail ourselves of God's available resources have been the major causes for good people losing their excitement over ministry. The resources God has for us can be all lumped under the term *grace*.

Grace Is the Secret

Paul is clear that the secret behind his unfading passion for ministry is not his own resources but the grace of God. He writes, "Therefore, having this ministry by the mercy of God, we do not lose heart" (2 Cor. 4:1). Here he uses a stronger word than grace, which has the idea of unmerited favor. Instead, he says, his ministry is because of "mercy" (*eleeō*), which has the idea of pity to a helpless person. Elsewhere he attributes his ministry to God's mercy (1 Cor. 7:25; 1 Tim. 1:13, 16), as well as to God's grace (1 Cor. 15:9–10; Gal. 1:15).

We all have weaknesses. Therefore, when we depend on our abilities, we become nervous and apprehensive as we give ourselves to the high calling of serving the almighty God. We might work hard and perform well, but we become insecure people. Grace is our great qualification for ministry, not our own skills and commitment. Paul says, "Not that we are sufficient in ourselves to claim anything as coming from us, but our sufficiency is from God" (2 Cor. 3:5). So while we work hard, we must rest in the promises of God.

If you are anything like me, you are often overwhelmed by your inadequacy to meet the demands placed upon you. But biblically speaking that feeling should be a source of freedom to minister. Paul found that the Lord's answer to his thorn-in-the-flesh problem was the sufficiency of grace: "My grace is sufficient for you, for my power is made perfect in weakness." Paul went on to say, "Therefore I will boast all the more gladly of my weaknesses, so that the power of Christ may rest upon me" (2 Cor. 12:9). Rather than being a source of embarrassment, his weakness became a reason for boasting. Grace frees us from the pressure to show off our abilities so that we can concentrate on showing off God's abilities. Rather than being a handicap to ministry, our feeling of weakness becomes a blessing because it prompts us to go to God helplessly, which in turn opens the door to grace coming into our lives. So Paul is able to say, "When I am weak, then I am strong" (2 Cor. 12:10).

I was thirty-seven years old when I had one of my biggest assignments as a speaker. I gave a plenary address at Billy Graham's Amsterdam '86 International Conference for Itinerant Evangelists. There were about ten thousand evangelists in attendance, and I was a bundle of nerves that morning. My stomach was upset, and I was going often to the restroom. My talk was the second one of the morning, and during the first talk I realized that I had to go to the restroom again. I rushed out and found a long line of people waiting to use the men's room. They kindly let me break the line, but I returned to the platform feeling quite miserable.

At the entrance to the platform, the program director, Dr. Leighton Ford, asked me whether there was a problem. After I shared my distress with him, he laid hands on me and prayed for me. Encouraged by his prayer, I had no feeling at all of nervousness as I spoke, and I was able to deliver my message with much freedom. Many who heard me said they were blessed, and had sensed no turmoil within me. My weakness became a source of great delight and thanksgiving.

Till the End of Our Lives

This grace keeps the glow of ministry going in our lives. Paul says, "Having this ministry by the mercy of God, we do not lose heart" (2 Cor. 4:1). God is faithful to his servants, and he provides them with sufficient grace to meet their daily needs. Therefore, we do not need to lose heart and think of giving up. We can trust God to faithfully provide all the spiritual, emotional, and physical needs for our life and ministry.

This grace will sustain us till the end of our lives. John Newton (1725–1807) was a converted slave trader who became a great minister of the gospel, campaigner against the slave trade, and hymnwriter. He often referred to his conversion as "the day I first believed," words that appear in his famous hymn "Amazing Grace" (1772). When he was dying, he told those around him that he was "packed and sealed . . . and waiting for the post." These were his last words: "My memory is nearly gone. But I remember two things: that I am a great sinner . . ." He paused for breath and then said, ". . . and that Christ—is a great Savior."[2] Grace was sufficient to the end. As Newton's hymn beautifully expresses it:

2   John Pollock, *Amazing Grace: John Newton's Story* (London: Hodder and Stoughton, 1981), 182.

Through many dangers, toils, and snares,
I have already come;
'Tis grace hath brought me safe thus far,
And grace will lead me home.[3]

Dr. Julian C. McPheeters (1886–1983) was in his late eighties when I was a student at Asbury Theological Seminary in the early 1970s. He was a retired president of the seminary and had come to live in an apartment on campus alone, as his wife had died many years earlier. He had a wide itinerant preaching ministry. In his forties he had suffered from a respiratory disease and was advised to keep himself physically fit. Even in his late eighties he was in better shape than most of us students. But what impressed us most was his preaching. He did not need a microphone. His voice boomed out his message, and when he preached expositorily, he would recite the whole Bible passage from memory. I often thought, *If I live to my late eighties, I hope I have such vitality and passion!*

A friend of mine who traveled with Dr. McPheeters told me something which I view as a secret of Dr. McPheeters's vitality. When he would get up in the morning, he would jump out of bed and quote Psalm 118:24 in a loud voice: "This is the day that the LORD has made. Let us rejoice and be glad in it!" He entered every day with the attitude that God was in control of the day ahead. That perspective enabled him to live each day anticipating the blessings that grace would bring.

In the pages that follow we will look at ways that can ensure that a constant supply of grace is being poured into our lives, and consider obstacles to this supply of grace.

---

3   John Newton, "Amazing Grace," 1779.

Keep Getting Grace Every Day

If grace is the key to life and ministry, then we should desire to be equipped with grace daily. And God promises that to us. As Lamentations 3:22–23 puts it,

> The steadfast love of the LORD never ceases;
>> his mercies never come to an end;
> they are new every morning;
>> great is your faithfulness.

Therefore, it should not surprise us that Paul begins all thirteen of his letters wishing his readers grace and peace. And Peter begins his letters with the wish, "May grace and peace be multiplied to you" (1 Pet. 1:2; 2 Pet. 1:2). The Greeks had a rather colorless salutation, *chairō*, which simply means "greeting." The characteristic Jewish greeting was *shalom*, which means "peace" in Hebrew. Early Christians substituted *charis* (grace) for *chairō* and added it to the Jewish greeting, yielding "grace and peace."

Just as Paul and Peter wished for their readers to experience grace, so we should thirst for grace daily in our lives too. The psalmists expressed this thirst as a thirst for God. A troubled psalmist said,

> As a deer pants for flowing streams,
>> so pants my soul for you, O God.
> My soul thirsts for God,
>> for the living God. (Ps. 42:1–2)

Another psalmist, probably David, wrote,

O God, you are my God; earnestly I seek you;
    my soul thirsts for you;
my flesh faints for you,
    as in a dry and weary land where there is no water. (Ps. 63:1)

The psalmists wrote these lines when they were experiencing great difficulty. Even when things seem to be going wrong, our main pursuit is God and his grace. Suffering becomes a blessing because it enhances our experience of grace, the most valuable thing in our lives. An article about healing in a dictionary of theology states, "God can use sickness and suffering to his glory and as a *means of grace* to men and women (Job 42:1–6; 2 Cor. 12:1–10)."[4] Instead of being preoccupied with our suffering, we view suffering as a means of experiencing deep and profound grace, which is one of the great desires of our life.

The Scriptures invite the thirsty to come and be satisfied. Isaiah says,

Come, everyone who thirsts,
    come to the waters;
and he who has no money,
    come, buy and eat! (Isa. 55:1)

Jesus invites, "If anyone thirsts, let him come to me and drink" (John 7:37). Of one who responds to that invitation, Jesus says, "Out of his heart will flow rivers of living water" (John 7:38). We become radiant, and our life and ministry are fresh with living water. So just as we pray for grace in our lives, we pray daily for

---

4 John Wilkinson, "Healing," in *New Dictionary of Theology*, ed. Sinclair B. Ferguson, David F. Wright, and J. I. Packer (Downers Grove, IL: InterVarsity Press, 2000), 287. Emphasis added.

the thirst which opens our hearts to receiving grace. Oh, may we never lose the taste for the glory and joy of grace.

A desire to receive more and more grace will drive us to open ourselves to grace through every helpful means available to us. We will incorporate into our lives practices that mediate grace, such as corporate worship, prayer, confession of sin, reading God's word, reading biblical, theological, and devotional books and biographies, and fellowshiping with others who are thirsting for God. My favorite practice is the singing of hymns. Even when I am burdened by problems and have no words of praise that spontaneously come from my heart, I can focus on the eternal realities of grace in the words of a hymnwriter. And this process is aided by music, the language of the heart. Music helps truth to travel the sometimes-long journey from the head to the heart. How important it is for us to pause our feverish activity and receive gracious refreshment from God.

John and Betty Stam, missionaries in China, were killed by Communist soldiers in 1934 when they were twenty-seven and twenty-eight years old. John once said, "Take away everything I have, but do not take away the sweetness of walking and talking with the king of glory."[5] Again, I say, may we never lose the taste for the glory and joy of grace.

Further Reflection

What things can you do to maintain a grace perspective to life, especially when things go wrong? In other words, how can you live each day anticipating the blessings that grace will bring? What things should you avoid doing?

---

5   Sherwood Eliot Wirt and Kersten Beckstrom, eds., *Living Quotations for Christians* (New York: Harper & Row, 1974), 266.

3

Strength for Energy-Sapping Ministry

I SOMETIMES RECEIVE gentle rebukes from my Western friends about working too hard.[1] I therefore have had to think a lot about the issue of hard work. Their contention is that the way I work can lead to burnout. My conclusion is that I need to be mindful of the dangers of working too hard. But I believe the fear my well-meaning friends have concerning hard work comes out of living in a fast-paced culture where success is often measured according to one's celebrity status. This can cause people to be driven to succeed according to false measures. The problem is compounded by personal feelings of insecurity, which we all live with.

These factors can cause people to be overdiscouraged by failure and slow numerical growth, to be possessive of their work so that they don't delegate duties to others, and to work without resting or observing the biblically mandated weekly Sabbath.

---

1   Some of the material in this chapter is presented in an expanded form in my book *The Call to Joy and Pain: Embracing Suffering in Your Ministry* (Wheaton, IL: Crossway, 2007), chaps. 28 and 29.

Such an unbiblical lifestyle inevitably results in burnout and excessive discouragement. My contention is that often burnout is not the result of hard work but of hard work that is driven by insecurity and false values.

Hard Work

Describing the work of nurturing mature disciples (Col. 1:28), Paul says, "For this I toil, struggling with all [Christ's] energy that he powerfully works within me" (Col. 1:29). Discipling is hard work. I wonder whether this is a reason why most leaders talk about the need for discipling in the church, but few are willing to pay the price of nurturing saints. Elsewhere, Paul says he experienced "toil and hardship, . . . many a sleepless night, . . . hunger and thirst, often without food, . . . cold and exposure" (2 Cor. 11:27). Today if ministers said things like that, they would be rebuked, perhaps advised to go for counseling, and even told that they are not aligned with God's good will for their life.

The verb translated "toil" (*kopiaō*) in Colossians 1:29 takes the meanings "work, work hard, labor . . . ; become tired, grow weary."[2] The corresponding noun is used by Paul autobiographically in 1 Thessalonians 2:9 and 2 Corinthians 11:27. It refers to physical exertion. I don't think Paul considered it a sin to be tired. When he was an old man, John Wesley (1703–1791) is reputed to have said that he was weary *in* the work but not weary *of* it. Doesn't it seem as though those we disciple experience problems at times when we are very busy? When our children have a serious problem, we cannot say, "This is not on my calendar for today." And our disciplees are like our children. More than once I have said something like,

---

2 Barclay Newman, *Greek-English Dictionary of the New Testament* (New York: United Bible Societies, 1971), 102.

"Why did he have to do this terrible thing *now*?" When our spiritual children need extra attention, we attend to them no matter how busy we are. Tiredness is the result.

Part of the toil that Paul describes in Colossians 1:29 is the ministry of the word (Col. 1:28). In our busy world, preparing for the ministry of God's word can be exhausting. We need to know the Scriptures, which are the key to the growth of people to maturity. Jesus said, "Sanctify them in the truth; your word is truth" (John 17:17). We also need to know about the kind of world that the people we minister to live in, as Paul did with the people of Athens (Acts 17:16–32). That is getting harder and harder to do as ideologies that are contrary to biblical teaching are getting more and more popular and accepted by society. The freedom to practice things we once called sin is now considered a human right. We have to understand our world and look for convincing reasons to demonstrate why biblical teaching is still valid. This is difficult in an age when people are enamored more by experience than truth. One result is that preaching is downgraded and "worship" is upgraded. We need to labor to bring back the high place of God's word in the Christian life.

In such an environment we need adequate time for preparation, but such time is difficult to find for anyone who is committed to nurturing people under their care. Dedicating time to both pastoral care and study is a challenge. The great Bible expositor and former pastor of Westminster Chapel in London, G. Campbell Morgan (1863–1945), was often asked to reveal the secret of his success. He would answer, "I always say to them the same thing—work; hard work; and again work."[3]

3 Jill Morgan, *A Man of the Word: Life of G. Campbell Morgan* (Grand Rapids, MI: Baker, 1972), 325.

Yet I must say that spending long hours preparing for the ministry of the word has been one of the most refreshing things in my life. There is something exhilarating about handling the life-giving word of God.

Of course, we must battle to get the rest we need. Yes, it is a battle to which we must apply ourselves with commitment. We don't want to hurt ourselves through exhaustion. So we work hard at finding times to rest amidst our busyness. We devotedly take our weekly Sabbath rest as an act of obedience to God. We are steadfast in our practice of spending time daily in the presence of God in prayer and with the word. We delegate work to others, and we nurture those who can take on more responsibility. We are not little messiahs who have to tend to every need that crops up. And, as we will see, God is committed to our welfare and will give us the rest that we need according to his timetable.

Listening to Warning Signs

One practice that helps us avoid the excesses of hard work is the habit of listening to warning signs. Sometimes our bodies send us messages of tiredness that we must take seriously. We might start to feel unusual weariness, listlessness, or irritability. If we go on and on working hard when we are fatigued, we can do our bodies and minds irreparable harm. I try to take a break from work when I sense that my body is protesting. It is dangerous to live in a perpetual state of emergency. We may need to push our bodies to an extreme for a short period. But that is an exception; it should not be our normal way of living. We must listen to our bodies.

I have also learned to heed warning messages from my wife and children. If our family is worried about our workload, we should take their warnings seriously. Often, because we are so immersed in our work, we don't realize the extent to which we are hurting ourselves and those around us. Our loved ones can notice the damage. I have seen too many examples of God's servants who disregarded their spouse's warnings on the grounds that they were obeying God's call. By the time they realized they were on a wrong path, serious damage had been done. The spouse who once was genuinely committed to ministry can become bitter over the damage the work has done to family life.

Because of this danger, we should talk regularly with our family members about our work schedule. We may be tempted to avoid such conversations when we fear they might be unpleasant. But regular conversations promote understanding on all sides and prevent the growth of bitterness over ministry. If you sense your spouse is upset, the natural reaction is to retreat. That can be disastrous to our marriages. Nurturing our families in their understanding of the work we are doing is a key responsibility of those in ministry.

Just as warnings from family members are helpful to us, so are warnings from accountability partners, close friends, supervisors, and counselors. Others often see dangers in our lives to which we are blind because we are so absorbed in ministry.

Struggle

The other verb Paul uses in Colossians 1:29 to describe the discipling ministry is translated as "struggling" (*agōnizomai*). It has the idea of battling or wrestling. We are engaged in a strenuous battle for people's souls. Now, it is true that battling for people's lives can be a key to freshness in ministry. It helps us keep alert spiritually, for we cannot lead others to holiness unless we also are holy. Sometimes when people I mentor talk to me about the temptations they struggle with, I realize that I encounter the same temptations.

I am alerted that I must be careful about my own life. Engaging in spiritual battle with God's strength and without neglecting other important aspects of life has a way of rejuvenating us spiritually. Even when my friends retire from paid ministry, I urge them to continue battling for people's souls through personal witness, prayer, counseling, and mentoring/discipling.

But battling for souls can also be spiritually and emotionally draining. Paul told the Galatians, ". . . my little children, for whom I am again in the anguish of childbirth until Christ is formed in you!" (Gal. 4:19). Elsewhere he said, "There is the daily pressure on me of my anxiety for all the churches. Who is weak, and I am not weak? Who is made to fall, and I am not indignant? (2 Cor. 11:28–29). Some disciples of Christ who have great potential are like rough diamonds, and before they are "polished" and mature, their disciplers will need to engage in a draining struggle. Some might say it is wrong to spend so much time and emotional energy on one troublesome person. But by dropping such a person, we may miss the opportunity to nurture a powerful and effective servant of God.

You might find yourself trying to restore a backslidden Christian who is resisting your intervention. You might be praying for deliverance of a person from demon possession. You might be battling to restore unity in your community. In evangelistic preaching, we are storming the gates of the kingdom of Satan. Just the act of preaching is a battle for people's attention and acceptance of the message. After such battles we can be physically, emotionally, and spiritually drained. Satan can hit us at such vulnerable times. I once read of a pastor who would visit a prostitute on Sunday evenings. Emotionally drained after a strenuous day of ministry, many of us would be more inclined to watch something impure on TV.

We need to be prepared for such vulnerable moments. We need to make plans for how we will face these challenges. I usually request to stay in homes when I am on preaching tours in the West. But that is not always possible. When I have to stay at a Western hotel, I text my wife and accountability partners informing them that I am in a hotel and that I will unplug the TV after about ten o'clock. Rarely does good come on the television after ten.

God's Energy and Power

While tiredness and struggle are inevitable in ministry, they do not need to be crippling. God's grace is sufficient so that, in keeping with the promise of Scripture, in the end all problems will have worked for our good (Rom. 8:28). God will be with us to guide us through each difficult challenge. Paul alludes to this when he says he toils and struggles "with all [Christ's] energy that he powerfully works within me" (Col. 1:29). The word *energy* (*energeia*) tells us that God provides strength to fulfill the calling to toil in ministry. The word *powerfully* (*dynamis*) tells us that he will provide the spiritual power we need when we are "struggling" for people's souls.

Energy for our toil and power for our struggles! There is provision for every challenge we face. Our task is to ensure that we are always obedient to God and his ways and that we keep tapping into God's unlimited resources by availing ourselves of the means of enrichment he has provided for us, including prayer, reading the Bible, community worship, and fellowship with other believers. Then we can trust God to provide us what we need.

Years ago I was getting ready to leave home at midnight on Christmas Day to go to America to speak at the Urbana Student Missionary Conference. I was nervous because I had been very busy and had lost sleep because of all the things I had to accomplish before Christmas. I was afraid that the fatigue and the jet lag would leave me so disoriented that I wouldn't be able to speak well at the conference. I was scheduled to preach at the Christmas service at our church on Christmas morning. I finished preparing the sermon at around two in the morning and went to sleep, hoping for at least four hours of sleep.

Shortly after I fell asleep, I heard a knock at our door. An infant in a poor Hindu family living near our home was sick with a stomach illness. They did not have electricity in their home, and in the low light from an oil lamp they mistook some skin lotion for the child's medicine, and accidentally fed him the lotion. When they realized their error, they came to our home hoping that we would take the child to hospital, which I did.

As the poor are sometimes neglected in government hospitals, I stayed with them until I was sure they had been properly cared for. By the time I came home, it was time to get ready for church. But I needed my sleep! I decided I would try to get some sleep after our Christmas lunch. We put our van in the garage and closed our windows, hoping people would think no one was at home. I had slept only for a few minutes when a visitor came. I went back to sleep, and a few minutes later I was woken up by another visitor. I decided that Christmas afternoon was not a good time to sleep! I played some games with my children instead.

But I still needed sleep! At midnight I went to the airport. The plane that took me from Colombo to Amsterdam had about three hundred and fifty seats, but only about fifty passengers. I had four seats to myself, which became a very comfortable bed. I have never slept on a flight as long or as deeply as I slept on that memorable Christmas night! God is able to provide the refreshment we need as we serve him. That is an aspect of the sufficient grace that he promises to us.

Further Reflection

Do you have people or practices that help alert you to possible imbalances in your schedule? Do you need to start some practices to ensure that you receive such alerts?

4

Thanksgiving and Joy

I HAVE COME TO NOTICE that the most joyful people in my life and ministry are also the most thankful, and joyous people experience freshness as they go about their service. We have seen that God's grace is a means of freshness over the long haul. *Thanksgiving* for that grace—and the joy that it sparks—also refreshes us in our ministry.

Thanksgiving

After talking about how God helped him during a terribly painful experience, Paul said, "But thanks be to God, who in Christ *always* leads us in triumphal procession, and through us spreads the fragrance of the knowledge of him everywhere" (2 Cor. 2:14). He says that those who are filled with the Spirit give "thanks *always and for everything* to God" (Eph. 5:20). Elsewhere Paul advised, "Give thanks in *all circumstances*; for this is the will of God in Christ Jesus for you" (1 Thess. 5:18). When we speak of doing the will of God, how often do we mention thanksgiving as part of it!

In the three texts above, I have emphasized the words that show that thanksgiving (and praise) are to be on our lips *all the time*. Later we will see that sometimes the attitude of thanksgiving comes only after we have grappled with God through groaning and lament. We must develop the habit of grappling with God when things go wrong until the perspective of grace breaks through into our lives. But after the grappling will come thanksgiving, so that the abiding sentiment in our lives is one of thanksgiving for God's grace.

Joy

The emotion that lies behind thanksgiving is joy. And joy is an important distinguishing mark of a Christian. Joy is an important Hebrew concept, given how many different terms there are for it. The Old Testament has thirteen "Hebrew roots used for some aspect of joy,"[1] which expands to twenty-three or more different words for joy. The theme of joy likewise pulsates throughout the New Testament. It begins with the announcement of the birth of Christ as "good news of great joy" (Luke 2:10), which leads to the naming of our message as the *gospel*—good news. British Reformer, Bible translator, and martyr William Tyndale (ca. 1494–1536) expressed his excitement over the gospel in the preface to his translation of the New Testament. He wrote that the word *gospel* signified "good, merry, glad and joyful tidings, that makes a person's heart glad, and makes him sing, dance and leap for joy."[2]

The Christian Approach to Life

The interconnectedness of the basic aspects of the Christian approach to life is well described in a discovery I made a few years

---

1   Clinton E. Arnold, "Joy," *The Anchor Bible Dictionary*, ed. David Noel Freedman (New York: Doubleday, 1992), 3:1023.

2   I have written this quote in contemporary English, from Robert Mounce, "Gospel," *Evangelical Dictionary of Theology*, ed. Walter Elwell (Grand Rapids, MI: Baker, 1984), 472.

ago of key Greek words that are etymologically based on the same Greek root: *char-*.

- The first word is *charis*, which is the grace that gives us salvation and results in us becoming God's children. This deals with the question of identity: we are children of God.
- Those who are saved by grace also receive gifts to use for God's glory. The word for such gifts is *charisma*. This gives us significance; we have work of eternal value to do.
- With the deep needs for identity and significance satisfied, we become contented people, resulting in an attitude of thanksgiving. The word for thanks is *eucharistia*.
- Thankful people are joyful people. The word for joy is *chara*.
- Out of the strength of joy we are able to give freely. That word is *charizomai*. *Charizomai* is sometimes translated "forgive" (Eph. 4:32; Col. 3:13). Grace makes us gracious, so that we have strength to forgive.

Charis	Grace
Charisma	Gift
Eucharistia	Thanks
Chara	Joy
Charizomai	Freely give, forgive

Service, then, is an overflow of the joy God has given us. We see this in Jesus's words in John 15:11–13. He says, "These things I have spoken to you, that my joy may be in you, and that your joy may be full" (15:11). With that joy we have the strength to give ourselves to sacrificial service. Jesus goes on to say, "This is my commandment, that you love one another as I have loved you.

Greater love has no one than this, that someone lay down his life for his friends" (15:12–13).

Joy Gives Us Strength

Ministry brings with it many blows. Most people in vocational ministry do not acquire great wealth or earthly honor. But if we are joyful people, we are rich! Joy gives us the strength to face trials and approach life with a positive outlook. Note that when Jesus spoke about giving his joy to the disciples, he was about to endure the most painful death anyone would ever face. Joy remained with Christ even as he prepared himself for his death.

I once heard David Sitton, founder of To Every Tribe Mission, tell a story from his teenage years. A ninety-year-old missionary spoke at the youth fellowship of his church. He had been a missionary for seventy-two years. At the start of his talk, the missionary kept saying the same thing over and over again. It was something like, "I want you to remember this. You can forget everything else I say, but don't forget this." He repeated this for a few minutes, and the young people were getting impatient, wishing that he would go ahead and say it. Finally, he said what he wanted to say: "The joy of the Lord is your strength. When the joy goes, the strength goes." Having said that, he sat down! He was quoting Nehemiah 8:10: "The joy of the LORD is your strength."

Paul presents the pursuit of joy as an imperative for the Christian. He says, "*Rejoice* in the Lord always, again I will say, rejoice" (Phil. 4:4). Joy is something we must actively pursue with perseverance. Once in a New Year's address George Mueller (1805–1898) said, "The welfare of our families, the prosperity of our businesses, our work and service for the Lord, may be considered the most important matters to attend to; but according to my judgement, the most important point to be attended to is this: *above all things to see that your souls are happy in the Lord.*" He went on to say, "Other things may press upon you; the Lord's work even may have urgent claims upon your attention" but this pursuit of joy is "of supreme and paramount importance. . . . Day by day seek to make this the most important business of your life."[3]

The joy of the Lord is a wonderful treasure. We must not leave home without it! If we always have this joy, we will have a positive attitude toward life. Then it is unlikely that the freshness of living and serving will leave us. No matter what may befall us, the roots of our renewal and strength are reliable and unchanging. A daily supply of refreshment is available to keep us enthusiastic about life and ministry.

Mueller launched into an itinerant evangelistic ministry at the age of seventy, which he continued until he was eighty-seven. During these seventeen years he traveled two hundred thousand miles, ministered in forty-two countries, and preached to about three million hearers. These figures are amazing considering that this was before the time of airplanes and sound-amplifying systems. When someone asked Mueller the secret of his long life, he gave three reasons. The third was the happiness he felt in God and his work. (We will mention the other two reasons—living with a clear conscience and refreshment from the Scriptures—in later chapters).[4]

Further Reflection

How are you involved in the battle for joy in your life? Should you be more proactive in engaging in this battle?

---

3 *Spiritual Secrets of George Mueller*, selected by Roger Steer (Wheaton, IL: Harold Shaw, 1985), 111–12. Emphasis in original.

4 *George Mueller: Man of Faith*, ed. A. Sims (Privately published in Singapore by Warren Myers), 51.

5

Three Reasons for Joy

IF THE JOY OF THE LORD is a key to freshness in service, then why do so many Christians who serve God, including those in vocational ministry, show little evidence of being joyful people? The disposition of some could be described as anger or disappointment more than joy. The apostle Paul probably faced more disappointments than most Christians. But his most joy-filled book, Philippians, was written from prison. From jail he wrote, "Rejoice in the Lord always; again I will say, rejoice" (Phil. 4:4). So what exactly do we mean by "the joy of the Lord"?

I believe the joy of the Lord is so multifaceted that we cannot express its full meaning in one simple definition.[1] Many features contribute to making joy what it is. But in the pages to follow, I will describe three foundational reasons for why we can have the joy of the Lord. Joy is the attitude with which we approach life because of these truths.

God Loves Us

The first reason for joy is the fact that God loves us. He loved us enough to send his Son to die for us. After stating that "we

1 For a discussion on this see my book, *The Call to Joy and Pain: Embracing Suffering in Your Ministry* (Wheaton, IL: Crossway, 2007).

rejoice in our sufferings," Paul says, "God shows his love for us in that while we were still sinners, Christ died for us" (Rom. 5:3, 8). The word translated as "shows" (*sunistēmi*) carries the idea of "proves" (NRSV).[2] Later in Romans, Paul uses a similar argument to give assurance that God will look after us: "He who did not spare his own Son but gave him up for us all, how will he not also with him graciously give us all things?" (Rom. 8:32). When things go wrong, we may be tempted to doubt that God truly loves us and cares for us. Even though we might believe this truth in our heads, we can let problems cloud out the reality of God's love. The truth alone that God loves us does not break through our circumstances and give us the joyous assurance that God will take care of us. The journey from the head to the heart is sometimes a long one. But it does not need to be so. We have proof: Jesus died for us.

Not only did Christ die for us, but he also saved us and made us his children. What an exhilarating thought! John was so thrilled by this fact that he exclaimed, "See what kind of love the Father has given to us, that we should be called children of God; and so we are" (1 John 3:1). Even those who have not had the privilege of having a trustworthy father have an image of what a trustworthy father should be like. God surpasses that image.

Some years ago, I was ministering out of town on my birthday. I came home after midnight, and when I went to my desk, I saw a card from my wife. I know that my wife is very careful about choosing the right card for an occasion. So after I read the beautifully affirming message, I thought, "This woman loves me." As I was basking in that fact, I was hit by another realization: "And God loves

---

2   See Thomas R. Schreiner, *Romans: Baker Exegetical Commentary on the New Testament* (Grand Rapids, MI: Baker, 1998), 260.

me even more!" But we frail creatures can forget that God loves us. So we need to go back to the proof: Christ died for us. As the familiar hymn by Jennie Evelyn Hussey expresses it, "Lest I forget thy Love for me, Lead me to Calvary."[3] Jesus knew our tendency to forget. This is why, when instituting the Lord's Supper, he said, "Do this in remembrance of me" (Luke 22:19).

The fact that we are beloved children of God can spark deep joy in our lives. But we must accept and believe that fact. Sadly, it seems that many Christians live as if they don't believe that God loves them. I consider Romans 15:13 to be one of the most important verses in the Bible about the Christian life. It describes how this joy can be a reality in our lives even when things go wrong: "May the God of hope fill you with all joy and peace in believing, so that by the power of the Holy Spirit you may abound in hope." Notice that hope is mentioned twice in this verse. Hope is looking up when things go wrong. God fills us "with all joy and peace." But how can we have joy in times of suffering? The second part of the verse gives us the answer: "in believing." We must believe that God loves us and will look after us. Exercising faith opens the door to joy.

We feed faith by reading the Bible. In my life God has also used songs to remind me of his unwavering love for me, which I am prone to forget in the midst of life's difficulties. Music, the language of the heart, can help truth to travel from the head to the heart. God also uses the encouraging words of others to feed faith. And when we spend time alone with God, grappling with the realities of our circumstances and God's unchanging truths, faith can be rekindled.

---

3 Jennie E. Hussey, "King of My Life, I Crown Thee Now," 1921 (Renewal Hope Publishing, 1949).

Self-pity helps buttress bitterness. It can be a dangerous companion. Self-pity is a good listener. While our brothers and sisters in Christ might give us godly advice that makes us bristle, self-pity will support us in our bitterness and anger. When tempted toward self-pity or bitterness over our circumstances, we must challenge those feelings with what we know about God's care for us. When everything seemed gloomy for the psalmist, and God seemed to be far away, he kept preaching to himself:

> Why are you cast down, O my soul,
>   and why are you in turmoil within me?
> Hope in God; for I shall again praise him,
>   my salvation and my God. (Ps. 42:5–6; see Pss. 42:11; 43:5)

We need to keep repeating the truths about God to ourselves to feed faith and attack unbelief. In his classic book *Spiritual Depression* Dr. Martyn Lloyd-Jones asked, "Have you not realized that most of your unhappiness in life is due to the fact that you are listening to yourself instead of talking to yourself?"[4]

Of course, when wronged, we must acknowledge that wrong has been done. Christianity does not advocate blind forgiveness. Jesus died a cruel death because a price had to be paid for sin. Injustice and unfair hurt are displeasing to God, and we should acknowledge that. We may have to seek justice for ourselves and for others. For example, when we have been defrauded, some process may be necessary to ensure that the wrong is not ignored. But we do not need to give nefarious people the honor of ruining our lives; that is an honor they do not deserve. But that is

---

4 D. Martyn Lloyd-Jones, *Spiritual Depression: Its Causes and Cure* (Grand Rapids, MI: Eerdmans, 1965), 20–21.

exactly what we do when we behave as if their influence on us is greater than God's.

Sadly, for some, unfortunate circumstances have become part of their identity. They hold tightly to injustices they have suffered. They provide an excuse for their anger and disappointment with life. It takes an act of faith to fight against self-pity and affirm that God is indeed in control of our lives. It takes faith to hold on to the truth that "for those who love God all things work together for good" (Rom. 8:28).

Here, then, is the first reason for the joy of the Lord: we are loved by God, who has saved us and made us his children. We allow that reality to impact us by believing. I have found this to be one of the most challenging aspects of discipling people. Some have experienced so much hurt in life that they find it difficult to accept that God really loves them and will always (through all circumstances) work for the good.

Jesus Is with Us

The second reason for joy is the fact that Jesus is always with us. Before he left this earth, Jesus promised, "Behold, I am with you always, to the end of the age" (Matt. 28:20). Shortly before he died, Jesus told the disciples, "So also you have sorrow now, but I will see you again, and your hearts will rejoice, and no one will take your joy from you" (John 16:22). The presence of Christ with us makes our joy inextinguishable even in the face of suffering. In fact, Paul talks about a special nearness with Christ that comes to us when we suffer because then we "share his sufferings" (Phil. 3:10). Because Christ is a suffering Savior, when we suffer, we enter into fellowship with him in a deep way. This depth of oneness with Christ is possible only through suffering. Fellowship with Christ is the sweetest thing in our life, therefore suffering becomes a source of joy. I was able to find twenty-one places in the New Testament where suffering and joy come together.[5]

This presence of Christ gives us the courage to face the greatest hardships. John Paton (1824–1907) left a comfortable life in Scotland with his young wife in 1858 for the New Hebrides Islands (now called Vanuatu). There his faith was severely tested as he faced a hostile people whose behavior did not seem to be even remotely close to accepted norms in the West. He wondered whether he had made the right decision to give "up [his] much beloved work and dear people in Glasgow, with so many delightful associations to consecrate [his] life to these . . . people."[6]

Three months after arriving, his wife and baby died, and he had to dig with his own hands the lonely grave where he buried them. He said, "I was stunned: My reason seemed almost to give way." But, he said, "I was never altogether forsaken. The ever-merciful Lord sustained me to lay the precious dust of my loved ones in the same quiet grave. But for Jesus, and the fellowship he vouchsafed me there, I must have gone mad and died beside that lonely grave."[7] Strengthened by the presence of Christ with him, Paton stayed on there for several years. He took a few years' break for raising support and people for this mission. Then, following his return in 1866, he saw most of the islanders turn to Christ.

---

5 Matt. 5:12; Luke 6:23; John 16:20, 22; Acts 5:41; Rom. 5:3; 12:12; 1 Cor. 12:26; 2 Cor. 2:2–3; 6:10; 7:4, 9; 8:2; Gal. 4:27; Col. 1:11, 24; 1 Thess. 1:6; Heb. 12:2; James 1:2; 1 Pet. 1:6; 4:13.

6 From Frank Cumbers, ed., *Daily Readings from F. W. Boreham* (London: Hodder and Stoughton, 1976), 320.

7 Cumbers, *Daily Readings*, 320.

The companionship of Christ brings a brightness to our life which enables us to be at peace amidst the most painful experiences. Indeed, I may weep deeply; I may be deeply disappointed. But even deeper down there is the assurance that God is with me. So the weeping is not hopeless and bitter. It acknowledges the loving presence of Christ. The assurance that God is with me sparks joy. I have come to realize that a mature Christian is able to have the joy of the Lord and a broken heart at the same time. The pain is intense, but the presence of Christ is an abiding, solid reality.

When I was a member of the Lausanne Committee for World Evangelization, I got to know a Scandinavian bishop, fellow member Hakon Anderson. He came to one meeting shortly after he had recovered from a serious heart attack. He shared that, as he was recovering in hospital, his son asked him whether he was thinking of God when he was close to death. His reply was, "I do not know whether I was thinking about God, but my only hope was that God was thinking about me!"

Our next cause for joy is knowing what is in God's mind when he thinks about us.

God Likes Us

The third reason for joy is the fact that God not only loves us— he actually likes us! In this competitive, angry, and impatient world, we experience a huge load of rejection from various sources: friends, family, colleagues, officials, teachers, competitors, enemies, and neighbors. Such rejection from so many areas can leave us wounded, feeling unloved and sensing the need to retrieve our dignity by whatever means we can find. We can become angry people. But the Bible delivers this startling message: God delights in us.

Scripture tells us that God "delights" or "takes pleasure" in us (Pss. 35:27; 41:11; 44:3; 147:11; 149:4; Isa. 62:4). Zephaniah 3:17 encourages us with exhilarating vividness: "The LORD your God . . . will rejoice over you with gladness; . . . he will exult over you with loud singing." The words we translate as "exult" and "loud singing" both have the idea of shouting for joy. One Hebrew lexicon says that the word translated "exult" carries the sense of to "shriek ecstatically."[8] Sometimes when we are thrilled, we shout or shriek for joy. That was what we did as a family in 1996 when we watched Sri Lanka win the Cricket World Cup. We all screamed for joy! How amazing it is to know that God regards us with such joy.

Affirmation is a remedy for the effects of rejection. And God is the most significant affirmer one could have. G. Campbell Morgan was considered one of the greatest preachers of his time. As a young candidate for the Methodist ministry, Morgan had to preach a trial sermon, and it did not go well. When the results were announced, he learned that he had failed. He sent a one-word telegram to his father: "Rejected." And he sat down and wrote in his diary, "Very dark everything seems. Still, he knoweth best." Quickly the reply came from his father: "Rejected on earth, accepted in heaven. Dad."[9] Braced by the knowledge of God's acceptance, Morgan did not give up thoughts of the ministry. He joined the Congregationalist Church and went on to become one of the greatest preachers of his era.

Knowing that God delights in us is cause for great joy in our lives, just as a child is thrilled to know that his parents are pleased

8   William L. Holladay, ed., *A Concise Hebrew and Aramaic Lexicon of the Old Testament* (based on the lexical work of Ludwig Koehler and Walter Baumgartner) (Leiden, Netherlands: Koninklijke Brill, 2000), 59.
9   Jill Morgan, *A Man of the Word: Life of G. Campbell Morgan* (Grand Rapids, MI: Baker, 1972), 57–60.

with something he has done. It also takes away the pain of the rejection we face on earth. The psalmist says, "Those who look to him are radiant, and their faces shall never be ashamed" (Ps. 34:5). When we look to God and receive his affirmation, the shame of rejection on earth is defeated. We may be rejected on earth, but we are accepted in heaven, the most elevated place of all.

———

The joy of the Lord is based not on what happens to us on earth, but on God and his attitude toward us. His love, his presence, and his delight in us give us reasons to be joyful, even during very painful moments. Even when we weep from pain and grief, we can find great solace and joy in telling ourselves, "God loves me. God is with me. And God delights in me."

We spend much of our time every day being faithful to God by fulfilling the responsibilities he has given us toward our families, our vocations, our neighborhoods, our nations, our organizations, and our churches. We must work hard at these God-given callings and conscientiously fulfill them. But all of our work should be undergirded by the fact that God loves us. Let us never forget that the most important thing about us is not what we do for God but what God has done and continues to do for us!

I am convinced that when people's general approach to life is one of joy, they are able to cope with all the challenges they face, however painful or severe, and remain contented with life. No problem can permanently take away the bedrock of joy that is foundational to their experience. If joy is not foundational, problems can take the upper hand and ruin our contentment. How I would like to plead with all my fellow workers in Christ's vineyard to fight for joy and not give up until joy becomes the general disposition of their lives.

Further Reflection

How will you make the truths that God loves you, is with you, and is delighted in you a reality in your daily life and thoughts?

6

When I Don't Feel Joy

WE KNOW THAT the joy of the Lord helps us to maintain freshness in ministry over the long haul. But some faithful Christians go through times when they experience the opposite of joy. We need to reckon with this fact when discussing the joy of the Lord.

Individual Personalities

Often these joyless periods are caused by specific tendencies within us that hinder us from experiencing a perfectly balanced life. The dispositions of some people influence their moods. Dr. Gaius Davies, who was a consultant psychiatrist at the famous King's College Hospital in London and a committed Christian, wrote a book, *Genius, Grief and Grace*, in which he discussed the lives of eleven of God's great servants. These believers, who had a mighty influence upon the church and the world, suffered from serious conditions such as anxiety and depression. They include Martin Luther, John Bunyan, William Cowper, Amy Carmichael, J. B. Phillips, C. S. Lewis, and Martyn Lloyd-Jones.[1]

---

1   Gaius Davies, *Genius, Grief and Grace: A Doctor Looks at Suffering and Success* (Fearn, UK: Christian Focus, 2001).

Bible translator J. B. Phillips (1906–1982) had a genius for writing and for translating God's word in a lively and attractive way. Over ten million copies of his books have been sold. His testimony as a translator, *The Ring of Truth*, had a major influence in the formation of my Christian convictions as a youth. But he had a disposition (somewhat connected to his upbringing and health problems) that made him susceptible to severe—and sometimes crippling—depression. Sometimes his depression would last for significant lengths of time.

Dr. Davies also mentions Martin Luther, that gallant warrior for grace, who took on the mighty Church of Rome, pressed home the importance of justification by faith, and became the most influential figure in the Protestant Reformation. Luther often suffered from depression and from severe symptoms of anxiety that resulted in panic attacks. This was true of Charles Spurgeon, as well, who said, "I am the subject of depressions of spirit so fearful that I hope none of you ever get to such extremes of wretchedness as I go to."[2]

William Cowper (1731–1800) is another of Dr. Davies's subjects. He was considered England's most popular poet for a time. He is the author of such well-loved hymns as "God Moves in a Mysterious Way" and "Hark, My Soul! It Is the Lord!" Cowper became a Christian after his first nervous breakdown and was afflicted with severe mental illness, off and on, after he came to Christ too. For many years he lived next door to and was cared for by John Newton (who wrote "Amazing Grace") and his wife. Cowper attempted suicide many times.[3] Shortly after writing "God Moves

---

2   Charles H. Spurgeon, "Joy and Peace in Believing," in *The Metropolitan Tabernacle Pulpit Sermons* (London: Passmore & Alabaster, 1866), 12:298–99.

3   See Jonathan Aitken, *John Newton: From Disgrace to Amazing Grace* (Wheaton, IL: Crossway, 2007), 206, 213, 218–19.

in a Mysterious Way," he relapsed into what one author called "madness."[4] Yet his hymns have ministered to many, including me.

Sometimes wounds inflicted on us cause us to live without joy in our lives. By wounds I mean such trauma as rape, sexual abuse, growing up in an abusive home, and being subjected to gross unkindness or unfairness. It has been my sad experience to counsel with several mature Christians who live with hidden rage over the wicked punishments meted out by parents. In our rushed world, where people experience high levels of anxiety, many become victims of the temper tantrums of stressed-out people. The victims of such rage then often react to unpleasant situations with rage of their own.

We are all weak, far from perfect, and struggling to live in a way that reflects God's perfection. Paul affirms that "God chose what is foolish in the world to shame the wise; God chose what is weak in the world to shame the strong" (1 Cor. 1:27) and "we have this treasure in jars of clay, to show that the surpassing power belongs to God and not to us" (2 Cor. 4:7). We know that perfection will be reached only in heaven.

Recent advances in medical and mental health studies give us a better understanding of some of our maladies. It would be wise to avail ourselves of these discoveries through counseling and other forms of medical treatment. Some people can experience a relatively high degree of healing. Some will live with their condition until they get to heaven. These are areas fraught with controversy. But the desire to be as healthy as we can be should drive us to seek help. Sadly, some people refuse to accept that they have a problem. Because they refuse to seek help, they end up hurting themselves, others, and the cause of Christ.

4   Aitken, *John Newton*, 218–19.

Before leaving this section, I will mention what has been called "the dark night of the soul," times when things have turned dark and gloomy and a person is confused and bewildered. Often this is the gateway to a new and deeper experience of God. Sometimes it lasts for a long time. Awareness of this phenomenon can enable an afflicted person to persevere in seeking God without giving up.

Seasonal and Circumstantial Maladies

Sometimes joy leaves us because of temporary circumstances. A good example is postpartum depression. According to the Mayo Clinic, "Most new moms experience postpartum 'baby blues' after childbirth, which commonly include mood swings, crying spells, anxiety and difficulty sleeping."[5] Women can also experience changes of moods during their menstrual period. Some sicknesses influence our emotions negatively. We might experience emotional lows after battling certain illnesses. Realizing what is happening helps us to get a handle on the pain, live with it realistically, and minimize the damage it might cause.

Overwork and the loss of sleep can trigger bad moods. When we realize this, we should listen to our bodies and prioritize rest. Continuing to work at an unrealistic pace when suffering symptoms of exhaustion can damage us permanently and, consequently, hurt those near to us. After the great battle at Mount Carmel, Elijah suffered from a severe attack of depression (1 Kings 19). Despite God's miraculous provision, Elijah kept saying that he wanted to die. God allowed him to spend many hours sleeping. Only after letting him rest for several days did God commission him with his next assignment.

5 "Postpartum Depression," Mayo Clinic website, https://www.mayoclinic.org/. Accessed October 8, 2022.

Guilt also has a way of taking away our joy. Guilt causes us to lose our peace and the blessing of sweet fellowship with God. When we do wrong, we need to respond as soon as possible, not only by asking forgiveness from God but also by confessing to those who have been hurt by our actions. Our spouses and accountability partners can also be agents of healing at such times. James said, "Confess your sins to one another and pray for one another, that you may be healed" (James 5:16).

Demonic Attacks

Battling forces of evil in explicit ways, like casting out demons, is commonplace in Christian ministry in my area of the world. And Satan continues to be alive and well in the West too. He can affect the emotions and thus the joy of Christians all over the world.[6] When Christians sense that their emotions are under attack, it is wise to ask whether a demonic attack is involved. Certainly, most attacks on one's emotions do not have a demonic origin, and it is harmful to classify primarily psychological maladies as demonic attacks. But some problems do have such a source. In such instances, concerted prayer by God's people is essential for deliverance from Satan's attacks.

While being careful about immediately concluding that a demonic attack is at work, we should always be open to that possibility. It would be wise to get the help of a person skilled in this sphere of ministry. Years ago, my wife and I ministered to a lady who, along with her family, was convinced that she was possessed by a demon. I took her to a minister who deals with such cases. After talking

---

6   See Timothy M. Warner, *Spiritual Warfare: Victory Over the Powers of This Dark World* (Wheaton, IL: Crossway, 1991) for a balanced, biblically grounded treatment of this issue. For a briefer description, see Warner's "Power Encounter with the Demonic," in *Evangelism on the Cutting Edge*, ed. Robert E Coleman (Old Tappan, NJ: Fleming H. Revell, 1986).

to her at length, he concluded that she was suffering from acute depression. Later events revealed that this was an accurate diagnosis.

Painful Family Circumstances

Throughout history, many faithful servants of God have lived with unhappy family situations. Many Christians have children who reject their parents' values and opt for a life of rebellion against God. Hosea had an immoral wife. John Wesley's wife tried to publicly discredit her husband. William Carey's first wife suffered from mental illness. I know a few good and godly pastors who are in difficult marriages.

Sometimes the difficult person in a marriage is the minister. Ada, the wife of A. W. Tozer, served the Lord as a faithful pastor's wife. But she had to live with a famous husband who did not know how to express his love for her or care for his family. After Tozer died, Ada married Leonard Odam. When people lovingly inquired about her happiness, she would say: "I have never been happier in my life. Aiden [Tozer] loved Jesus Christ, but Leonard Odam loves me."[7]

When the people who are supposed to be closest to us cause us deep pain, our joy in the Lord is severely tested. We live with constant pain in our heart. Yet despite these sorrows, many great Christians have persevered in their work effectively and continued to find their satisfaction in God. Sometimes God used the pain they endured to make them great servants for his kingdom. For instance, Hosea's love for his adulterous wife helped him to understand God's love for his disobedient people. Other painful family situations involve caring for loved ones who suffer from severe physical diseases or mental illness. God's servants are not immune to the challenges

---

7   Quoted in Lyle Dorsett, *A Passion for God: The Spiritual Journey of A. W. Tozer* (Chicago: Moody, 2008), 160.

faced by the rest of humanity. Those who face such are honored by God, for he enables them to bear such burdens.

We must do all we can to help reduce the burdens of such families. And we must be careful not to make insensitive judgments about the situations these people face and their responses to them.

Living with Pain

Some Christians live within situations where joy seems to be impossible. Even to such, the truth of Romans 15:13 applies: "May the God of hope fill you with all joy and peace in believing, so that by the power of the Holy Spirit you may abound in hope." Our hope is that while grappling with huge physical, spiritual, emotional, or mental challenges, we may still keep trusting God so that deep down, amidst the gloom, we can still say, "I know that I am God's child, and I know that he is with me." Then, while feelings of happiness may be missing, the basis for joy is still intact and we have peace in the midst of gloom. This peace moderates our actions by guarding our hearts and minds (Phil. 4:7) and ruling in our hearts (Col. 3:15). In other words, peace helps us respond to difficult situations without harming ourselves or others.

I like to tell myself and others: *don't feel bad about feeling bad*. God is still with us!

Further Reflection

Are you or others you know experiencing some of the exceptional situations described in this chapter? If so, what can you do to assist yourself or others to cope with your/their difficult circumstances?

7

The Reality of Frustration

THE PRECEDING CHAPTERS have given us strong reasons for being joyful amidst the difficulties and disappointments we face in life and ministry. Yet most devout Christians struggle when they face painful experiences. The Bible has a place for such struggle. Most Christians have been exposed to a strong emphasis on the blessings God gives us without a corresponding emphasis on the *reality of disappointments* in life. Disappointment over the disappointments one faces can dampen joy even among faithful believers. In the next three chapters, we want to build a biblical-theological foundation for facing hard times.

In the first four chapters of the apostle Paul's most theologically systematic book, the epistle to the Romans, he expounds on the way of salvation by grace through faith. After a summary statement about the way of salvation in the first two verses of chapter 5, he makes a statement about suffering: "Not only that, but we rejoice in our sufferings" (Rom. 5:3). Chapters 6–8 deal with the issue of holiness, climaxing in a statement about life in the Spirit (8:1–17a). That discussion on sanctification leads to a powerful exposition on suffering (8:17–39). So after explaining both salvation and sanctification, Paul talks about suffering. A theology of suffering, then, is key to understanding the Christian life.

I have written a whole book that explores the theology of suffering devotionally.[1] In the next two chapters I will discuss three aspects of the theology of suffering from Romans 8, which I believe will enable us to accept suffering with contentment without being disillusioned about what we are experiencing.

Frustration

Paul makes an affirmation about the reality of frustration: "For the creation was subjected to futility, not willingly, but because of him who subjected it, in hope" (Rom. 8:20). As a result of the fall, the world lost its equilibrium, and God himself subjected it to frustration. The word we translate as *futility* (or *frustration* in the NIV) is *mataiotēs*, which means "the inability of something to fulfill its intended purpose."[2] Things go wrong. This is the same Greek word that the Greek translation of the Old Testament, the Septuagint, uses in Ecclesiastes, which we translate today as "vanity" (ESV) or "meaningless" (NIV).

A distinct feature of the understanding of frustration in Romans 8 is the hope of God's ultimate victory. But while we are here in this fallen world, we will live with frustration. Indeed, God answers prayer and we have the authority of Christ in our lives and ministries. But our model is an incarnate Lord who "humbled himself by becoming obedient to the point of death, even death on

---

1   Ajith Fernando, *The Call to Joy and Pain: Embracing Suffering in Your Ministry* (Wheaton, IL: Crossway, 2007).

2   James R. Edwards, *Romans*, Understanding the Bible Commentary Series (Grand Rapids, MI: Baker, 2011), 213.

a cross" (Phil. 2:8). The author of life became obedient to death! Hebrews 2:10 says, "For it was fitting that he, for whom and by whom all things exist, in bringing many sons to glory, should make the founder of their salvation perfect through suffering." Our model is an incarnate Lord who suffered.

Several years ago, I did a study on New Testament references to Jesus as an example for Christians to follow. I found twenty-nine passages in the New Testament where Jesus is presented as our model. Six passages are general calls to be, to obey, and to forgive like Jesus. The other twenty-three passages are calls to suffer, to be servants, or to persevere with patience like Jesus. Most of the servanthood passages are about suffering. So twenty-three out of twenty-nine passages that ask us to follow Christ's example have to do with servanthood and suffering! To be like Jesus is to be willing to suffer.[3]

Therefore, we should not be surprised when we suffer while doing ministry, and we should not be discontented by our lot. I would say that a key requirement for anyone hoping to do ministry using the incarnational model of Christ is the ability to live with frustration.

Consider these examples of frustration. We proactively seek to win the lost, but few are saved. Some walk away from the faith and end up finding fault with the very person who labored to disciple them. People we trust betray us. Colleagues turn against us. People whom we help sacrificially turn against us when we do one thing that they don't like. Our spouses don't fully understand what our thinking is on many issues. We struggle with knowing how to parent our children well. An open-air program we worked hard to prepare for falls flat because of an unexpected rain shower. Plans for

3 See Ajith Fernando, "Jesus: The Message and Model of Mission," *Global Missiology for the 21st Century: The Iguassu Dialogue,* ed. William D. Taylor (Grand Rapids, MI: Baker Academic, 2000).

a fruitful year of ministry are ruined by a cancer diagnosis. People don't seem to understand who we are and what our motives are. Some don't appreciate our service and just try to grab whatever they can from us.

Pain from Those We Serve

Let's look at one area of frustration that causes pain to servants of Christ: rejection by those we serve. Paul's epistles often show him grappling with a sense that after all he had done for his readers, they had rejected his teaching for that of unworthy false teachers. He expresses his pain over this in Galatians and in 2 Corinthians. For example: "Make room in your hearts for us. We have wronged no one, we have corrupted no one, we have taken advantage of no one. I do not say this to condemn you, for I said before that you are in our hearts, to die together and to live together" (2 Cor. 7:2–3). Paul makes himself vulnerable as he opens his heart to his brothers and sisters in Corinth. He tells them, "We have spoken freely to you, Corinthians; our heart is wide open. You are not restricted by us, but you are restricted in your own affections. In return (I speak as to children) widen your hearts also" (2 Cor. 6:11–13).

If we open our hearts to the people we serve, as Paul did, the pain of rejection will be intense. Most people look at life from the perspective of their own needs and desires. If we fail to meet those needs, they will be dissatisfied. They will forget all the good we have done to them. They won't think about possible reasons why we did not do what they wanted. It may not matter to them that we were tired, or sick, or handling a family emergency. When we don't act in the way others want, they might blame us for that.

Often those we minister among do not appreciate us, while others outside our ministry seem to show more appreciation. This should not surprise us. When you are a leader, those you lead expect things from you. Most people are grumblers by nature. Guess whom they will grumble most about. Their leaders! It's easy for people to blame their leaders for not getting the things they want. Often there is some truth in what they think. We all make mistakes. And we expect others to appreciate the sacrifices we make for them. But sometimes people forget about all of that and complain that their desires have not been met. Recently, a person I had ministered to substantially called me after he heard me speak to accuse me of not practicing what I preach in my relationship with him. That was a hurtful blow!

Moses had to endure much grumbling from the people of Israel. Hebrews says of him: "By faith Moses, when he was grown up, refused to be called the son of Pharaoh's daughter, choosing rather to be mistreated with the people of God than to enjoy the fleeting pleasures of sin. He considered the reproach of Christ greater wealth than the treasures of Egypt" (Heb. 11:24–26). But the people whom he served faithfully and sacrificially constantly grumbled against him.

Some of God's great servants were rejected by the very people among whom they served. Jonathan Edwards (1703–1758) was possibly the greatest philosophical mind in North America. Under his leadership the church in America experienced a great revival called the Great Awakening. But Edwards was dismissed by the church he pastored! Of course, today he is considered a hero by many. New editions of his writings are presently being published, more than two-and-a-half centuries after his death.

Helen Roseveare (1925–2016) was a brilliant and heroic missionary doctor in the Congo. After graduating from Cambridge University, she went to the Congo and started a hospital in an area where there were no medical facilities. The demand for her services was so great that she started a program to help train others to treat patients. During a rebellion against colonial rule, she was repeatedly beaten and raped. She went back to the United Kingdom for a few months to recover, and then returned to the Congo. After some time she encountered a wave of anti-Western sentiment that affected even the Christians. This resulted in her being told to leave the work she started because she was no longer wanted there.

Yet, today she is considered to be one of the missionary heroes of the twentieth century. After her return to Britain, she began an international speaking and writing ministry. God also used her to bring healing to others who had gone through abuse as she had. I had the privilege of being with her at two conferences. The second time was when she was in her eighties. She was such a joyful and humorous person, certainly a testimony to the joy of serving the Lord.

I need to say here that, if our ministry is our primary source of fulfillment, rejection by those we serve can be a devastating experience. The behavior of other humans should never be the most important thing that we think about. Our primary fulfillment comes from God and his acceptance of us as his beloved children. If that is the case, then while rejection by humans is painful, as it was to Paul, it does not devastate us. Our deep source of joy is untouched by human rejection.

Our Frustration Is Mixed with Hope

Hope is a key theme in Romans 8. In Romans 8:20 Paul asserts that "the creation was subjected to futility . . . in hope." The next verse describes this as the hope of God's victory at the end of time: "The creation itself will be set free from its bondage to corruption and obtain the freedom of the glory of the children of God" (8:21).

Next Paul says, "The whole creation has been groaning together in the pains of childbirth" (8:22). Birth pangs represent hopeful groaning amidst pain. Later Paul says that hope prompts us to be patient amidst hardship (8:25). The Bible is clear that there is reward for faithful service. This gives us the courage to persevere. After describing the hope of our resurrection, Paul says, "Therefore, my beloved brothers, be steadfast, immovable, always abounding in the work of the Lord, knowing that in the Lord your labor is not in vain" (1 Cor. 15:58).

The Christian hope of rewards following the judgment is a key to contentment while facing injustice and unfair treatment in life and ministry. Being made in the image of God, we chafe against injustice. We may need to do something to redress the wrong done to us and others. But whether that works satisfactorily or not, we know there will be a reward for patient service. This frames our approach to life. So we think about the future consummation all the time and derive our values from there. As missionary C.T. Studd famously wrote:

Only one life, 'twill soon be past,
Only what's done for Jesus will last.

Some may have to wait until they get to heaven before they see their reward. Jeremiah was rejected by his people, and he suffered emotionally because of that. He was called a traitor. A main reason for this rejection was that he urged the people not to make an alliance with Egypt. The last we hear of him is that he himself was taken to Egypt. But there too he continued his ministry.[4]

---

4 "Jeremiah," *Baker Encyclopedia of the Bible*, ed. Walter E. Elwell (Grand Rapids, MI: Baker, 1988), 1112.

Other servants of God will see the fruit of their labors in this life. The Corinthians hurt Paul deeply by their unfaithfulness. He sent them another stern letter, which we do not have with us today. But this is what he says about that letter: "For I wrote to you out of much affliction and anguish of heart and with many tears, not to cause you pain but to let you know the abundant love that I have for you" (2 Cor. 2:4). He was so nervous after sending the letter that he couldn't do any work until news came of how the letter was received. He says, "When I came to Troas to preach the gospel of Christ, even though a door was opened for me in the Lord, my spirit was not at rest because I did not find my brother Titus there. So I took leave of them and went on to Macedonia" (2:12–13).

Then Paul got the good news from Titus that the church in Corinth had accepted the rebuke and repented. Thinking about that, without even mentioning that Titus had come, Paul burst into a chorus of praise: "But thanks be to God, who in Christ always leads us in triumphal procession, and through us spreads the fragrance of the knowledge of him everywhere" (2 Cor. 2:14). In this case Paul saw positive fruit during his lifetime.

Many believe they have obeyed God conscientiously but are encountering severe frustration and pain. Listen to the words of Paul: "And let us not grow weary of doing good, for in due season we will reap, if we do not give up" (Gal. 6:9). We always have hope that we will see rewards, either in this world or the next.

Further Reflection

How do you maintain a healthy balance between loving people in a way that includes openness to being hurt and ensuring that your primary sources of fulfillment are not your circumstances or the people you serve?

8

Groaning and Lament

WE ENDED THE LAST CHAPTER affirming from Romans 8:20–21 that frustration is inevitable in life and ministry, but that this frustration is mixed with hope. Paul describes what frustration mixed with hope prompts us to do: we groan. Both believers in Christ and creation itself groan under the weight of a fallen world.

Frustration Gives Rise to Groaning

We don't usually respond to trials immediately with joy. Often we first go through a process of acknowledging the pain. So we groan to God. Paul says that the creation groans as it awaits its redemption: "For we know that the whole creation has been groaning together in the pains of childbirth until now" (Rom. 8:22). The pains of childbirth are severe, but we know that they lead to the birth of something wonderful.

Like creation, servants of Christ also suffer pain. Paul goes on to say, "And not only the creation, but we ourselves, who have the firstfruits of the Spirit, groan inwardly as we wait eagerly for adoption as sons, the redemption of our bodies" (Rom. 8:23). Here the groaning anticipates the consummation: the redemption of our bodies.

Of course, Paul says, "we have the firstfruits of the Spirit." We have experienced God's sweet presence with us. We have seen him answer prayer and experienced his joy and power. We have had a taste of heaven, which Paul calls firstfruits. A person once was asked, "Do you expect to go to heaven?" He replied, "Why, I live there!" The presence of God with us is like heaven on earth. His joy and peace are sufficient to keep us fulfilled and contented. And yet we still face frustration on earth.

While he was on earth, Jesus also experienced frustration. He once said, "O faithless and twisted generation, how long am I to be with you? How long am I to bear with you?" (Matt. 17:17). But the most vivid example is in the garden of Gethsemane. It was a lonely time for Jesus, so "he took with him" his three closest disciples: Peter, James, and John. And Jesus "began to be greatly distressed and troubled" (Mark 14:33). He told them, "My soul is very sorrowful, even to death. Remain here and watch" (14:34). But three times he came to them, and he found them asleep! That same evening Jesus prayed, "Remove this cup from me" (14:36). But he submitted to God's will. That prayer did not receive a positive answer. Then Judas betrayed him, other disciples fled, and Peter denied knowing Christ.

How Jesus responded to these pains can be described as groaning. Luke says, "And being in an agony he prayed more earnestly; and his sweat became like great drops of blood falling down to the ground" (Luke 22:44). Jesus's groaning is revealed when he quotes a psalm of lament from the cross: "My God, my God, why have you forsaken me?" (Matt. 27:46; see Ps. 22:1).

Lament Is a Biblically Mandated Expression of Groaning

Though our worship rarely includes lament, at least one-third of the psalms in Israel's book of worship, the Psalms, have been classified as laments. Some scholars put that figure as high as half the psalms.[1] It is the largest category in the book of Psalms. When we are hit with something painful which we cannot explain and it seems as though God has not helped us, the Lord has given us permission to express our pain, doubts, and complaints. Mark Vroegop has described lament as "a statement of faith."[2] He says, "Lament is how you live between the poles of a hard life and trusting in God's sovereignty."[3]

Old Testament scholar Chris Wright describes the content of a biblical lament like this: "God I am hurting; and God, everyone else is laughing. And God, You are not helping very much either; and how long is it going to go on?"[4] David described lament as something that results from trust in God:

Trust in him at all times, O people;
    pour out your heart before him;
    God is a refuge for us. (Ps. 62:8)

Lament does not ensure that our problems will be solved immediately. But in keeping with the birth pains idea, lament is an affirmation of faith. It places God at the forefront of our thoughts. As Vroegop writes, "Lament is the song you sing believing that *one day* God will answer and restore."[5]

Lamentation can take different forms. Earlier we considered Jesus's words of frustration over the slowness of the "faithless and

---

1   That was the view of a beloved late scholar and editor at Zondervan, Verlyn Verbrugge.
2   Mark Vroegop, *Dark Clouds, Deep Mercy: Discovering the Grace of Lament* (Wheaton, IL: Crossway, 2019), 26.
3   Vroegop, *Dark Clouds*, 21.
4   Chris Wright, "Personal Struggle and the Word of Lament," in *Truth on Fire: Keswick Ministry 1998*, ed. David Porter (Carlisle, Cumbria: OM Publishing, 1998), 29.
5   Vroegop, *Dark Clouds*, 33. Italics his.

twisted generation" to respond to the truth (Matt. 17:17). Jesus wept over Jerusalem and lamented their rejection of "the things that make for peace," and the terrible consequences of their disobedience:

> And when he drew near and saw the city, he wept over it, saying, "Would that you, even you, had known on this day the things that make for peace! But now they are hidden from your eyes. For the days will come upon you, when your enemies will set up a barricade around you and surround you and hem you in on every side. (Luke 19:41–43; see 13:34–35)

Paul expresses similar sorrow over the rejection of the gospel by the Jews: "I am speaking the truth in Christ—I am not lying; my conscience bears me witness in the Holy Spirit—that I have great sorrow and unceasing anguish in my heart. For I could wish that I myself were accursed and cut off from Christ for the sake of my brothers, my kinsmen according to the flesh" (Rom. 9:1–3).

Hannah lamented not having a child (1 Sam. 1). As she wept in prayer in the house of God, Eli the priest did not understand what she was doing and rebuked her because he thought she was drunk. Many women desiring to have children express their sorrow in similar ways. And clearly God approved of Hannah's lament.

Lament also has an important place in the Old Testament records of funerals (Gen. 37:34; Deut. 34:8; 2 Sam. 1:17; 2 Chron. 35:25; Jer. 9:17-20; Amos 5:16).[6] That tradition carries over into the New Testament church. Acts 8:2 says, "Devout men buried Stephen and made great lamentation over him." After the death of Dorcas, "all the widows stood beside [Peter] weeping and showing

---

6 See my *Deuteronomy: Loving Obedience to a Loving God* (Wheaton, IL: Crossway, 2012), 390–91, 700.

tunics and other garments that Dorcas made while she was with them" (Acts 9:39). Perhaps public expressions of sorrow could help answer critics in Asia, who say that Christians dishonor the dead by the gaiety of their funeral rituals.

Lament can be a step in the healing of our sorrowing. Expressing our sorrow and weeping can help us dispel bitterness over what has happened to us, if the weeping is done in the presence of God. Joseph endured intensely bitter experiences. His brothers plotted to destroy him. He was sent to prison for being faithful to his master and refusing to have sexual relations with his master's wife. The fellow prisoner whom Joseph helped forgot about him. Yet he shows no sign of bitterness. We see his faith in God when he acknowledges God's sovereignty in his brothers' treachery, which gave Joseph freedom to forgive them (Gen. 50:20). Genesis 43–50 records Joseph weeping eight times.[7]

Vroegop reminds us that no one taught us to cry. That is the first thing we did when we "left the warm and protected home of [our] mother's womb." He says, "Tears are part of what it means to be human."[8] Tears mixed with faith open us to express our pain to God in lament, which in turn begins a process whereby faith brings the assurance of God's sovereignty over our situation.

We should not insist that everyone lament in the same way. Personalities differ. Some people are expressive by nature and do not have difficulty expressing their pain. Some share their pain with a few trusted people. Some weep alone. Some share their pain with God and leave it at that. But some bottle up their feelings and refuse to express any emotion. That can be dangerous and lead to bitterness or depression.

7 Gen. 42:24; 43:30; 45:2, 14, 15; 46:29; 50:1, 17.
8 Vroegop, *Dark Clouds*, 25, 38.

A word of caution: it is possible to dwell so much on our problems that we refuse to be open to God's healing. Once a period of lament is over, we must get back to work. When Sarah died, we are told that "Abraham went in to mourn for Sarah and to weep for her." After that period was completed, he went to work purchasing property as a burial site for his family: "Abraham rose up from before his dead and said to the Hittites, 'I am a sojourner and foreigner among you; give me property among you for a burying place, that I may bury my dead out of my sight'" (Gen. 23:2–4).

Of course, we need to be sensitive here and not insist on too heavy a burden of work too soon. But working is one way in which healing can come to us. I have encountered Christians who were active in ministry who went through a painful experience. Some suffered disappointment in love, or a bad experience related to ministry. Some have said, "I have served others enough. Now I must look after myself." And they stepped away from ministry. I think that is healthy for a short period of time. But they need to get back to working for the Lord. "The love of Christ controls" a Christian (2 Cor. 5:14). That word *controls* has the idea of applying pressure. God's love, "poured into our hearts through the Holy Spirit" (Rom. 5:5), cries out for release. And when we release it in service to others, we can find refreshing streams of healing.

Groaning versus Grumbling

We must say something about the difference between groaning and grumbling. Groaning is the cry of obedient people who are suffering despite their faithfulness. Grumbling is the complaint of those who don't want to be obedient or submit to God's will. They may not like the new pastor or leader, and they continually find fault with him. They may not like the people of one race or class, and they look for ways to show that they are given preferential treatment. Grumblers may be unhappy or bitter people who refuse to be patient with the weaknesses and actions of others and keep expressing anger over what is happening. Such people hurt themselves and the community to which they belong.

Groaning Is an Alternative to Quitting

In today's mobile culture people often change jobs. Many view long-term commitment as a thing of the past, and this has affected their attitude to Christian community. When problems come, people leave their church or organization without going through the pain of working for a resolution. Churches split when the differences between factions become too contentious. God's servants can simply move away because of problems they no longer want to face.

Sri Lanka has gone through crisis after crisis, making life difficult for its people. Some Christians leaders who have strong personalities and were examples of determination to complete tasks have left our country because they could not handle the frustrations of working in a broken nation. They found the challenges of incarnational ministry too difficult.

Many people I have discipled or mentored were what I call rough diamonds. They came from backgrounds where the Christian lifestyle looks strange. They made many mistakes and often brought shame to their discipler. But I often saw a spark of sincere commitment to God, which gave me hope. Some of these people are influential leaders today. I groaned many times over their behavior. But I did not quit on them.

Groaning sometimes comes from the people against the leaders. Leaders need to accept this as something that simply comes with leadership, even within the Christian community. We need to listen to the groanings of our people, which can be an unpleasant experience. One of the first community problems in the church recorded in Acts related to the groaning of church members. Acts 6:1 says, "Now in these days when the disciples were increasing in number, a complaint by the Hellenists arose against the Hebrews because their widows were being neglected in the daily distribution." The word translated "complaint" (*gongysmos*) is called an onomatopoetic word, where the sound suggests the sense carried by the word. The word sounds like the buzzing of bees.[9]

Something unpleasant was going on. If the leaders had dismissed the complaint as being the product of a rebellious group, the result would have been a division in the church on ethnic grounds. But the leadership acted on it immediately. By doing so they prevented a split, maintained the unity of the church, and instituted a new order of ministers in the church that became known as deacons. There was a healthy response to the groaning of the people. The leaders did not condemn them for their attitude, though it may have not been ideal. The problem was taken seriously, and the church was able to move on and grow. Immediately after this story Luke says, "And the word of God continued to increase, and the number of the disciples multiplied greatly in Jerusalem, and a great many of the priests became obedient to the faith" (Acts 6:7).

Because of our belief in the sovereignty of God, we are not afraid of pain and problems. They may hurt deeply. But we do not give up on God. We go to God and express our pain. We groan, we weep, we lament, and we receive his comfort and the strength to continue serving him.

9   I got this insight many years ago from Ralph Earle, *Word Meanings in the New Testament*, vol. 2, *John–Acts* (Grand Rapids, MI: Baker, 1982).

Further Reflection

How do you apply the biblical principles of groaning and lament when you face painful experiences? What should you do to prevent your groaning from deteriorating into grumbling?

9

The God Who Groans

SO FAR WE HAVE ASSERTED that frustration is an inevitable aspect of life in a fallen world. But this frustration is colored by hope (Rom. 8:20). This mixture of frustration and hope elicits in us hopeful groaning as in the pains of childbirth (8:22–23). Then Romans 8:26 presents the startling truth that *God also groans*. This reality is a key to our maintaining joy amidst pain.

The Holy Spirit as Helper

Paul says, "Likewise the Spirit helps us in our weakness. For we do not know what to pray for as we ought" (Rom. 8:26). When perplexed by situations that we cannot explain, we feel weak, and we don't know what to pray for. When unjustly attacked by someone, what do we pray for? How do we explain to others why their accusations are wrong? Can we ask God to teach them a lesson? How should we publicly respond to people who have hurt us greatly? When we are suddenly hit by a serious illness, should we change doctors? Can we in faith ask God for a miraculous healing? Should we have surgery?

Different devout and wise friends and relatives will give different answers to such questions. We feel weak, and we don't know how to pray. Paul says that in such situations "the Spirit helps us in our weakness." The word translated "helps" (*synantilambanomai*) is what is called a double compound. Three words come together to form this one word. It literally means "takes share in," which yields the idea of "to lend a hand together with."[1] A. T. Robertson explains, "Here beautifully Paul pictures the Holy Spirit taking hold at our side at the very time of our weakness."[2] It is as if our weakness is a heavy log, which is difficult to carry alone. We carry one end, and the Holy Spirit carries the other.

The Spirit shares our burdens. This fits with the role of the Holy Spirit as helper. John used the word *paraklētos* for Jesus's description of the Holy Spirit (John 14:16, 26; 15:26; 16:7). This word literally means "called (*klētos*) to be beside (*para*)" us.

Paraklētos has been translated as "advocate (NIV)," "Helper (ESV)," "Comforter (KJV)," and "Counselor (CSB)." When we feel helpless and weak, the Holy Spirit comes alongside us and lifts us up and helps us to go on. We don't bear our burdens alone. God does not simply throw down sufficient grace from heaven. He comes alongside us and helps us.

The Holy Spirit as Intercessor

Paul goes on to say that "the Spirit himself intercedes for us with groanings too deep for words" (Rom. 8:26). We groan under the weight of our weakness, not knowing what to pray for. The Holy Spirit comes alongside us and takes up our prayers and makes them

1 A. T. Robertson, *Word Pictures in the New Testament*, vol. 4 (Nashville TN: Broadman Press, 1933), on Romans 8:26.
2 Robertson, *Word Pictures*.

his own. Paul says that though we do not know what the will of God is, the Holy Spirit and God are on the same page: "He who searches hearts knows what is the mind of the Spirit . . ." (8:27). As the Spirit intercedes for us, he does so in keeping with the will of God. Paul continues, ". . . because the Spirit intercedes for the saints according to the will of God" (8:27).

Paul makes the amazing claim that the Holy Spirit acts as a divine editor and brings our prayers to accord with God's will. We may be praying for the wrong thing. But God knows our hearts, and the Holy Spirit intercedes for us, reconciling our prayers with God's will.

I ministered in South Africa in the late 1970s toward the end of the apartheid era. There was a civil war going on. I was impressed by the devotion with which the Christians I met prayed for God's intervention. When the war ended, the result was not what some of them had prayed for. The country transitioned to majority rule. Most people thought that there would be a bloodbath if such a transition took place. But under the new president, Nelson Mandela, that did not happen. I saw the prevention of further carnage as God's answer to the sincere prayers of Christians, some of whom had prayed for a different outcome.

Sri Lanka has endured a three-decade-long war, a bloody revolution, a devastating tsunami, and now an economic collapse. Throughout the more than forty years during which we have borne these crises, Christians have prayed. But often people wonder whether their prayers are making a difference. We don't even know what to pray for. We take heart believing that God knows what is happening and that he will use our prayers to be part of the solution to the problems.

So amidst the confusion we face in our weakness and our inability to get a handle on the situation, we are encouraged to pray. We know that we are God's children, and that he has our best interests in mind. His will "is good and acceptable and perfect" (Rom. 12:2).

The God Who Groans

But this will of God is not some distant perfection that we must reluctantly bow down to. It is the will of one who is close to us, who understands and cares for us. Hebrews 4:15 says this about Jesus: "For we do not have a high priest who is unable to sympathize with our weaknesses, but one who in every respect has been tempted as we are, yet without sin." Jesus understands the temptations we go through, including the temptations to despair and to look for an easy way rather than going down the hard path of obedience.

Now we come to a startling statement Paul makes in Romans 8:26. He says, ". . . the Spirit himself intercedes for us with groanings too deep for words." We've seen that the whole creation groans, and that we who have "the firstfruits of the Spirit, groan" (Rom. 8:23). Now we are told that the Holy Spirit groans. We are in pain; we feel weak and helpless. And he comes alongside us as our *paraklētos* and identifies so much with us that he groans with us. Our pain becomes his pain. This is a God who weeps, who understands our suffering.

Here is another antidote to bitterness. Often the closeness of a friend who understands us and remains with us in our pain is what helps heal us from bitterness and despair. What if that friend is God himself? We can expect a full and deep ministry to our lives from him. Today many hardworking Christians are bitter. They have been faithful, but they are not joyful. They have been hurt, but through sheer determination they have overcome their obstacles. "I'll show them that I can make it despite all their wickedness," they say. They do make it—and they succeed. But they lack the beauty that comes from being loved by a comforting God.

Others find themselves facing problems that seem impossible to solve. But they groan to God in their pain. And they realize that God groans with them. They enjoy the sweet privilege of experiencing the fellowship of sharing in Christ's sufferings (Phil. 3:10). They experience God's love in double measure. This experience of love banishes bitterness. They come through their pain comforted. Part of the sufficient grace that God gives is love that is strong enough to help us overcome bitterness (2 Cor. 12:9).

In the summer of 2011, I went to Bangor in Northern Ireland to preach at a missions convention. Just before I left for the trip, my wife, Nelun, had a biopsy to check for breast cancer. The doctor assured us that it was a routine test, and that we need not worry. While I was in Bangor, about fifteen minutes before I went to preach, my wife called to convey the test results. She had cancer! Later we found that it was a fairly virulent strain. But for the moment I pushed aside the implications of my wife's news and preached my message.

I was staying in a home close to the beach. That evening I went to the beach to spend some time with God. Using the Bible app on my phone, I meditated on Psalm 46 for an extended time. When I went to bed that night, I found myself weeping. Here my dear wife was alone at home in a time of crisis while I was thousands of miles away! Suddenly, the thought came to me: *I am weeping to God! Though I am so far from my wife, God is with us both.*

Nelun had to go through surgery, chemotherapy, and radiation. It was a difficult time for us. Thank God, she has been cancer free for more than ten years. During that ordeal, this thought often came to me: "Where would we be without Jesus?" He is with us in our groanings, and he is able to comfort us! We don't have to go through life with bitterness or despair. His presence with us and his love bring a sweetness that is deepened through suffering.

Further Reflection

Are you adequately accessing the comfort of the God who groans in your times of weakness? How can you apply the truth that God helps us in our weakness as you think of your own weaknesses?

10

Refreshment through Prayer

ONE ESSENTIAL PRACTICE that helps prevent burnout is having a consistent daily time alone with God, which must include prayer. Many things could be said about prayer, but in this chapter I will focus on demonstrating how spending time with God in prayer refreshes us and helps us respond to triggers of burnout.

Prayer Slows Us Down

One of the most debilitating effects of our rushed pace of life is its tyranny over our lives. We can go on working like workaholics until we drive ourselves to the ground. But, as we saw in chapter 3, the work of nurturing mature Christians involves toil and struggle (Col. 1:29). Working hard is not the problem. Working without stopping to rest and engaging in things like spending time with family, ministering to individuals, studying, and praying is the problem. The inability to stop and spend time alone with God could be a symptom of a serious spiritual malady.

The best way to address this problem is by deciding to stop and be still—even though that goes against our natural inclination.

Charles Spurgeon said, "I believe that when we cannot pray, it is time that we prayed more than ever. And if you answer, 'But how can that be?' I would say, pray to pray. Pray for prayer. Pray for the spirit of supplication. Do not be content to say, 'I would pray if I could.' No, but if you cannot pray, pray till you can."[1]

Prayer is an antidote to many of the problems busy people face. One of the benefits of praying is that it slows us down. The psalmist says, "Be still, and know that I am God" (Ps. 46:10). Slowing down amidst the physical and mental tiredness that result from facing challenge after challenge and fixing our gaze on God has a way of renewing our strength. When we set apart nonnegotiable time for prayer, there is no need to hurry during the prayer time—no matter how busy we might be. While the world rushes on, we can relax in the presence of God and find healing from the effects of a rushed life. Isaiah says,

> They who wait for the LORD shall renew their strength;
>> they shall mount up with wings like eagles;
> they shall run and not be weary;
>> they shall walk and not faint. (Isa. 40:31)

We are made to commune with God. That is an essential feature of authentic humanity. But we can block out that part of our life through excessive activity and through bondage to the digital world. One way to restore and affirm the priority of communion with God is to cease from busy activity in order to give ourselves to being alone with God. So Jesus said, "When you pray, go into your room and shut the door and pray to your Father who is in secret" (Matt. 6:6).

---

1 Charles Spurgeon, *The Metropolitan Tabernacle Pulpit*, vol. 24, 1877 (repr., Pasadena, TX: Pilgrim Publications, n.d.), 258. Cited in *Spurgeon at His Best*, comp. Tom Carter (Grand Rapids, MI: Baker, 1988), 143.

Prayer Helps Us Handle Painful Blows

We will all inevitably receive painful blows while serving God, which can drain our spirits and take away our freshness. When people attack us after we have sincerely tried to do what is right, we can feel deeply hurt. Being with God during these time helps us to gain perspective as we look at problems from God's point of view.

David wrote Psalm 27 when he was in deep trouble. Even his parents seem to have deserted him. Yet he was confident that God would not reject him. He wrote,

> For my father and my mother have forsaken me,
>   but the LORD will take me in. (Ps. 27:10)

He knew there was an open invitation from God to go to him. He said,

> You have said, "Seek my face."
> My heart says to you,
>   "Your face, LORD, do I seek." (27:8)

David made seeking God his preoccupation during his time of pain. He said,

> One thing have I asked of the LORD,
>   that will I seek after:
> that I may dwell in the house of the LORD
>   all the days of my life,
> to gaze upon the beauty of the LORD
>   and to inquire in his temple. (27:4)

The vision of the beauty of God can combat the impact of the ugliness we experience in ministry and free us from bitterness. I have always operated on the principle that when there is a disagreement within our team, we will grapple with it until we come to a consensus on how to proceed. But about thirty years ago Youth for Christ had a crisis and our leadership team was divided. Two sides saw two different ways out of the problem. However much we talked about it, we could not come to an agreement. Staff on both sides were upset with me, their leader. It was painful to see people I considered my children so upset with me.

Unable to lead by my usual "be of one mind" method, I felt that the only way I could lead was through prayer. So I would occasionally simply sit in my room at night for hours in an attitude of prayer. I was deeply distressed, but most of the time I had nothing to say to God. But I was conscious of the fact that I was near to him. Sometimes I would sing a hymn. When my heart felt some relief, with the sense that I had cast my burden upon the Lord (Ps. 55:22; 1 Pet. 5:7), I would go to sleep, knowing that God was with me.

One night I was up until about three in the morning. Later, after just a few hours of sleep, I had to teach a group of our staff and volunteers. A colleague came up to me just before I started teaching and poured out his heart about how disappointed he was. It was a hard pill to swallow just before speaking. But braced by the strength of knowing that God was with me, I was able to teach. I think the session went well.

During this crisis, I learned a principle that I still try to follow: during a crisis or conflict, before meeting with people, first meet with God. What we choose to do should not first be a response to what people say or do to us. Though that is important, it is easy to make mistakes when we act primarily in response to other humans.

Our work should first be a response to a call from God. We must meet every situation with the confidence of knowing that God has sent us and is with us. That confidence often comes from lingering in the presence of God. With that confidence we can avoid extreme reactions that can aggravate problems. Paul talks about the peace of Christ ruling in our hearts (Col. 3:15). The conscious presence of Christ with us moderates our behavior, attacks our bitterness, and prevents us from doing harm.

I praise God that after a long, hard struggle we were able to resolve the issues in our ministry in a God-honoring way without breaking our friendships.

Intercession Brightens Our Lives

As we grow in our Christian walk, we will invariably find ourselves spending most of our prayer time on intercession. James wrote, "The prayer of a righteous person has great power as it is working" (James 5:16). Praying might be the most powerful work we do. Paul mentions praying for his recipients in ten of his thirteen letters. For his spiritual child Timothy, to whom Paul had entrusted the care of the church in Ephesus, he prayed "night and day" (2 Tim. 1:3).

Praying for others is an act of love. When we pray, love is going out from us to others. But when we pray, we are also in communion with God, who is the source of love. Our hearts are open to God, and love comes in from God's inexhaustible resource of love. Love is going out of us and coming into us. In other words, love is fully activated in our lives. In and out! In and out! And we begin to glow with the brightness of the Lord. A lifestyle of care and concern for others without replenishment will leave us drained and empty. We must first experience God's love, and only then can we healthily give it out. As John said, "We love because he first loved us" (1 John 4:19).

Indeed, intercession is hard work. Paul describes Epaphras as wrestling in prayer for the Colossians (Col. 4:12). Those who have many people to care for will find themselves spending a considerable amount of time praying for them. This is hard, time-consuming work. Paul Rees was a popular Bible expositor and writer when I was young, and some of his books influenced me greatly. Someone once asked him whether he liked writing. His answer was, "It is good to have written." Writing is hard work, but when you have done it, there is a great sense of relief and joy. It is the same with prayer. Intercession is hard work, as we painstakingly pray for the people God has laid on our hearts. But once you have done it, a sense of joy comes over you. Love becomes activated in you and flows through you.

Get into the Habit Now

I must confess that I am not the most disciplined person. It is not natural for me to stick to routines. I am not proud of this weakness, and I sometimes suffer loss because of it. But there is one thing I have tried to do with consistency, despite this weakness, these past sixty years or so: having my daily time with God. Why? Because I know that if I neglect this time, I am finished! There would be no hope for me. It would be sheer folly not to have a consistent time with God in prayer.

Prayer is a habit. Usually I don't experience much excitement or emotional highs during my time with the Lord. But I still do it because I know that I am spending time with the Father whom I love and am reading the word he has given to me. Does not the Bible say, "Draw near to God, and he will draw near to you" (James 4:8)? I have never regretted persevering with prayer and Bible reading, even when no warm feelings emerged.

Many of us do not have nine-to-five jobs. We work till late at night on some days and start early in the morning the next day. Having a daily time with God can be a challenge with such a schedule. So each day, before I go to bed, I decide what time I will have my devotions the next day. If for some reason I need to change that plan at the last moment, I decide then and there what time I will do it that day. I consider my time with God to be the most important thing I do every day.

Of course, we do not need to be legalistic about having our devotional time. God is not going to strike us down if we miss this time occasionally. Though the Bible describes a disciplined routine of prayer in the lives of some of its heroes, like Daniel, it does not legislate procedures for daily devotions. But considering how prone we are to missing this time, it is good to have a strict watch over our schedules to ensure that we have a time with God daily. We do not have laws stating that we must have our physical food in a certain way. But we make sure that we eat every day. We can adopt the same approach to spiritual food. And considering the refreshment that we experience described above, we will not view this discipline as a burdensome duty.

I know that sooner or later I will get to the point where, for physical reasons, I will be too weak to have an active ministry in the traditional sense. But I will still be able to minister through prayer. Retirement then will be a promotion, so that I can concentrate on doing the most powerful thing we can do: pray.

But don't wait until you are old to get into the habit of lingering with God in prayer. Perhaps your busy life has caused you to neglect this means of grace, so that even when you do have the time, you don't automatically get into it. Once when I traveled with a few Christian leaders, we had an unplanned overnight stopover which led to a totally free night and morning. That morning, some in our group grabbed the opportunity to spend extra time with God. I believe that there were others who did not devote any time at all for this. I think they had lost the taste for prayer and Bible study. So don't wait till you retire to get into the habit.

There has been a revival of group prayer in Sri Lanka recently. I thank God for that. But I wonder whether there is a corresponding commitment to personal prayer. I think this is a problem all over the world. Let me urge you to develop a system by which you can ensure that you have a significant daily time devoted to prayer.

Further Reflection

Are you satisfied with your prayer life? What steps do you need to take to improve it?

11

Battling Insecurity

ONE OF THE MAIN CAUSES of burnout is insecurity. The struggle with deep insecurities can drain our spirits and make us seek fulfill-ment in unhealthy ways. Insecurity is the result of being unsure of ourselves and our place in life, which results in deep-seated shame about who we are.

We live in a world where competition is a way of life, and we grow up feeling that, if we are to succeed, we must do better than others. In their effort to motivate us to succeed in life sometimes parents, teachers, and bosses compare us to others. The result is that we get used to thinking of our performance in comparison with how others fare. And of course, we can always find people who do better than us in many things; therefore we aren't able to fully enjoy the fruit of our labors. These challenges are compounded by the fact that all of us have weaknesses, and our attitude to those weaknesses can influence the way we view ourselves.

I believe I am right in saying that all of us live with insecurities, though it is a bigger problem for some than others. Our response to this problem is important to our life and ministry.

How Insecurity Can Influence Our Life and Work

Insecurity expresses itself in different ways in different people, including how we approach life and work. Some are crushed by the negative messages they have received in life, and they lose their motivation to excel. Some settle for mediocre performances. Some struggle with discouragement, self-doubt, or depression. Some respond to the pain they have faced in life with anger; they are easily annoyed and prone to respond with unwise hostility in difficult situations.

Some respond to their insecurities with a determination to overcome obstacles and prove their worth by succeeding in life. This certainly is the best of the responses we have mentioned. Many such people become leaders in the church and in society. They work hard, and their commitment results in them being given positions of leadership. But if they don't handle their insecurities properly, the consequences can be dangerous.

- Some work too hard in their quest for success. Living an unbalanced life, they neglect their family and other responsibilities. Those close to them are upset by their workaholism. Because those close to them are unhappy, they too become unhappy. Hard work along with discontent is a dangerous combination. Such people drive themselves into the ground with overwork. Their unhealthy lifestyle catches up with them, often resulting in burnout. The joy of ministry and energy to persevere dwindles.
- Some do not delegate. They take on too many responsibilities, with unhealthy consequences. Ultimately that kind of leadership stifles healthy growth of a church or organization.

- Some are driven by unhealthy ambitions and ignore the welfare of colleagues in their quest for success. They may be threatened by others and do not make good team members because they see others as competitors. On their climb to the top, they have likely stepped on a lot of people.
- Some express their insecurity by exercising too much control over other people. Recently I have read of an alarming number of founders of large, well-known, and thriving movements who have been fired by the movement they founded because the body felt they were exercising too much control over people. People complained of a toxic organizational culture. This can become a serious problem in organizations like the one I work for, which places a strong emphasis on discipling. Disciplers take responsibility for the nurture of others. But as Peter warned, leaders should not be "domineering over those in [their] charge" (1 Pet. 5:3; see also 2 Cor. 1:24). Our authority is that of servants (2 Cor. 4:5). Insecure leaders prefer to control people more than serve them.
- Some have uncontrollable disappointment when they are overlooked for a promotion. Their status in the organization is so important to them that they take it as a personal blow when they don't get a position they want. I have seen Christians with bright futures resign from their jobs because they were angry at being overlooked for a promotion. After that they struggled vocationally for a long time and did not settle into something that fit their abilities.
- Some overreact when they have negative experiences. They respond with too much anger or discouragement when they experience failure, or when they are criticized, or when

their work is not recognized and appreciated, or when their ideas are rejected. Their insecurity makes them too weak emotionally to respond to such blows to their ego in a healthy manner.

- Some, desiring attention and affirmation from people other than their spouses, engage in extramarital affairs. I've heard people say things like, "How could he have abandoned his attractive wife for his unattractive secretary?" He worked very hard and often came home late. His wife was annoyed over this and often scolded him when he came home. At the church where he served as pastor, his secretary treated him like a god! He began to enjoy her company too much, and the result was an affair. Many years ago I read an article in my local newspaper on why religious leaders and politicians were susceptible to extramarital affairs. One of its main points was that these leaders who had worked hard and climbed to the top were still insecure children inside, yearning for affirmation. Engaging in illicit behavior with someone other than their spouse gave them the affirmation they craved.

- Youth workers can find too much satisfaction from their young people and not prepare them to be released from the youth program when they become adults. Many drop out from the church completely once they pass their youth years because they have not been thus prepared.

- Youth workers also have the temptation to enjoy the adoration of the young people they work with, especially youths from the opposite sex. Some become like the father the youth never had. What started as a helpful relationship can cross the line of propriety, and the result is an inappropriate relationship.

Prayer Attacks Insecurity

Prayer is one of the best means to overcome insecurity. When we spend time with God, we are communing with the one who is greater than any other entity, the one who rules the universe. The experience of being in the presence of this God and realizing that he is our loving Father who delights in us is the most powerful weapon to attack our sense of insecurity. As Deuteronomy 33:27 puts it:

> The eternal God is your dwelling place,
>   and underneath are the everlasting arms.

That is security.

As we bask in the secure love of the supreme God, the shame of our insecurity is challenged. David said, "Those who look to him are radiant, and their faces shall never be ashamed" (Ps. 34:5). While the shame described here was the shame coming from a crisis David faced, we can extend the application to all kinds of shame in our lives, including the shame of insecurity. Seeking God and sensing his affirmation through his answers to our prayers brings the brightness of God's security onto our faces.

When I was a theological student in the United States, John Stott visited our seminary. A short while before that he had visited Sri Lanka and befriended my parents. I went to every meeting that Stott addressed. After one meeting, he came up to me and asked, "Do I know you, Brother?" I replied that he did not know me, but that he knew my parents. I told him who my parents were. His response was to joyfully hug me. For the next few days I floated a few feet above ground level as I walked. My hero had hugged me!

I subsequently got to know John Stott and worked with him on a few projects. I was struck by his humility and his self-effacing nature. If I told him about my elation over being hugged by him, I suspect he would have told me, "Who is John Stott in comparison with God?" Being in the presence of our loving heavenly Father provides us with the greatest security! And that is what prayer is: being in God's presence.

We Need a Biblical Understanding of God

Of course, we won't be able to overcome our insecurities if we do not have a biblical understanding of who God is and respond appropriately to that understanding. We can summarize the nature of God with the term *holy-love*.

Because God is holy, he desires holiness from us. He says, "You shall be holy for I am holy" (1 Pet. 1:16; see Lev. 11:44–45). We cannot have fellowship with God if we continue in sin. John says, "If we say we have fellowship with him while we walk in darkness, we lie and do not practice the truth" (1 John 1:6). And, "Whoever says he abides in him ought to walk in the same way in which he walked" (2:6; see also 2:4; 4:20). When I led Youth for Christ, I sometimes would learn that a staff worker would get angry at the slightest provocation. I would ask myself two questions: "Is this person working too hard and not getting enough sleep?" and "Has this person fallen into a serious sin?"

Thank God, in Christ he has lovingly provided forgiveness for our sin. So when we repent and seek his forgiveness in prayer, he will "abundantly pardon" (Isa. 55:7), on the merits of Christ's death. I love that word *abundantly*! There is no hesitancy on God's part to welcome a repentant sinner. So Jesus taught that when we pray, we must ask God to "forgive us our sins" (Luke 11:4). Confession of sin is a regular part of a Christian's life.

Not only does God forgive our sins but he also forgets them. People may not forget, and that can be painful and embarrassing. But the most important entity in our lives, God, says, "I will remember their sin no more" (Jer. 31:34). Paul describes the consequence of forgiveness well when he writes, "There is therefore now no condemnation for those who are in Christ Jesus" (Rom. 8:1). Without this freedom from condemnation, we would lose our security. Therefore, confession ought to be a major segment of our prayer life.

This seems almost too basic a matter to write about. Sadly, however, many Christian workers forfeit the freedom of a warm relationship with God by refusing to acknowledge their sin. Even the great King David struggled with this. He said that when he "kept silent" about his sin, his "bones wasted away" (Ps. 32:3). In chapter 13 I describe how lack of confession blocks grace in our lives. I know of Christian workers who have committed serious sins in the areas of sex or money, but their guilt could not be proved. Though it was clear to many that they were guilty, the offenders avoided being disciplined. Sometimes they were transferred to another place of service, where they would commit the same sins over again.

When I fail in areas related to my weaknesses, I share my failure with my accountability partners. This is in keeping with James 5:16: "Confess your sins to one another and pray for one another, that you may be healed." That accountability along with their prayers is helpful for healing me after failure and serve as an incentive to avoid a recurrence of the sin. Two Greek words for confession (*homologeō* and *exomologeō*) are used five times in connection with confessing sin (1 John 1:9; Matt. 3:6; Mark 1:5; Acts 19:18; James 5:16). In every case, the context is the community of believers. God intends for us to grow in holiness along with other Christians. As we shall see when we discuss the role of friends in our lives (see chap. 18), corporate discipline is enacted as a treatment for our weakness as a step toward healing.

Freed from the insecurity that guilt causes, we can enjoy the blessings of God's love. Foremost among these is the privilege of being adopted as God's beloved children. This is a fact that John marveled over. He said, "See what kind of love the Father has given to us, that we should be called children of God; and so we are" (1 John 3:1). The Bible even says that God delights in us.

> He will rejoice over you with gladness;
> . . . he will exult over you with loud singing. (Zeph. 3:17)

This is the glorious gift of love that God gives us: the thrill of knowing not only that God loves us but also that he delights in us.

We are constantly bombarded with ideas that challenge the reality that God is holy-love. These lead to unbelief, cynicism, fear, and erratic behavior. Therefore, when we pray, we must remind ourselves of the unchanging realities about God that are more significant than the negative messages we receive from this world. Praising God helps us do that. I have a pastor friend who sends me a hymn every morning. I usually start my daily time with God by singing that hymn. Adoration and praise through song is a good way to reorient our minds to focus on the unchanging realities about God.

Understanding who God is heals us of the pain, rejection, and shame we experience on earth. And we confirm the truths of God as we spend time with him.

Other Antidotes to Insecurity

A sense of true security may not come all at once to a praying person. In fact, some people who spend a lot of time in prayer have very unpleasant natures and show many signs of being insecure people. There are other means that may be necessary for overcoming insecurity.

First, many who have come to Christ as wounded people first experienced *acceptance through the loving Christian community* that welcomed them into its fellowship. By receiving acceptance from fellow Christians, they had tangible evidence that they were acceptable people. That opened them to the thought that God also would accept them. Many of God's blessings to us are mediated through the body of Christ. Security is one of these. There is great security in having a group of friends who accept us and are willing to pay the price of being our friends. In our highly mobile society, where people change churches, homes, and jobs regularly, having long-lasting friendships has become a challenge. But it is an essential feature of the life of a secure person. I deal with the topic of friendship in the last two chapters of this book.

Sadly, the Christian community can be a place that also inflicts deep hurt upon its members. Unlike God, the community is not a perfect source of security. We must labor to ensure that people find their primary fulfillment in God and not the community.

Second, through involvement in the body, *we realize that we have been gifted* for the service of God. As we begin to exercise our gifts and see God using us, we are given a fresh message that we have a significant role to play in his kingdom agenda. Realizing our significance is a powerful way to attack insecurity. Knowing that I had been called to serve God was a key to helping me handle my sense of inferiority and discouragement over my weaknesses.

Third, *the counsel of friends or qualified counselors* can also help heal us of our insecurities. Knowledgeable people can pinpoint areas of insecurity in a person's life and lead the way to healing. Some think there is a stigma attached to going for counseling, and they avoid doing so. That is unfortunate, considering how much pain they could avoid for themselves and for others.

Total security will be realized only when we get to heaven. Until then we must remain alert regarding our insecurities and take steps to reduce the damage they can cause. And as we open ourselves to God's healing, little by little God ministers his affirmation to us, and the truth breaks through into our lives: I am a beloved child of the ruler of the universe.

I love the image of a child, frightened by a barking dog, running to her mother and clinging to her. In the warmth of her mother's embrace, the child experiences security. That's what we do when we are battered by rejection and other challenges to our sense of security. We cling to God our Father.

Further Reflection

Given the reality that everyone grapples with insecurity, it would be good to list the sources of insecurity in your life. How might you prevent the problems that can come from these insecurities?

12

Guarding Our Integrity

BECAUSE EXPERIENCING God's grace (or mercy) is the key to maintaining freshness in ministry, we should want to remove all hindrances to receiving that grace. When we act in ways that are contrary to God's principles, we block his grace, and therefore we resort to doing God's work in our own strength. In my youth I read a statement that I have never forgotten: "The hardest work to do is the work of God in your own strength." Doing spiritual ministry in our own strength will sap our energy and leave us weak and unmotivated. We also lose the great accompaniment of grace in our lives: the joy of the Lord, which is a key to maintaining freshness.

After mentioning that he does "not lose heart" because his ministry is "by the mercy of God," the apostle Paul states that lack of integrity is a hindrance to grace (2 Cor. 4:1). This passage shows that integrity and conscience are clearly connected to not losing heart, or remaining fresh, in ministry. Paul says, "But we have renounced disgraceful, underhanded ways. We refuse to practice cunning or to tamper with God's word, but by the open statement of the truth we would commend ourselves to everyone's conscience in the sight of God" (2 Cor. 4:2). Integrity is important to Paul.

Renouncing Disgraceful Ways

Paul presents negative and positive aspects relating to integrity. Negatively, he first says, "But we have renounced disgraceful, underhanded ways." It is shameful ("disgraceful") to break our principles. Often we can climb in society and in the church by violating God's principles. But such behavior is shameful to us. We are princes and princesses in the mighty kingdom of God. This is how Paul describes our status: "If then you have been raised with Christ, seek the things that are above, where Christ is, seated at the right hand of God. Set your minds on things that are above, not on things that are on earth" (Col. 3:1–2). Because we have been raised to such heights, acting without integrity is below our dignity.

Others may succeed by hurting others, by neglecting the weak, by spreading gossip, by telling lies, by engaging in unethical financial practices, and by breaking the law. But such behavior is below us as God's children. God does not need for us to stoop to using the methods of Satan to win his battles. We "set [our] minds on things that are above." This gives us a perspective that enables us to overcome temptations to use wrong methods for success. Besides, the most fulfilling thing in life is knowing that God smiles upon us. When we lose that smile, we lose the joy of the Lord—which is a great treasure. We can guard this joy by seeking to live in a way that pleases God. Of course, we all fail along the way. But we have God's forgiveness that comes with repentance, which restores the joy of the Lord in our lives.

Refusing to Practice Cunning

Second, Paul says, "We refuse to practice cunning" (2 Cor. 4:2). The Greek word translated *cunning* literally means "the readiness to do anything."[1] We are often tempted to do things that break God's principles in order to succeed. Some will crush others or spread bad stories about their competitors. Some will give gifts to people, even in the church, to win their support in an election. Some will hide a serious sin because, if the sin were to come out, the whole ministry might crash. This kind of behavior is common in pragmatic cultures. If people are successful, others don't make much of a deal about the methods they used to achieve their success.

Garry Trudeau, creator of the *Doonesbury* comic strip, once said, "There is something disturbing in our society when men wish not to be esteemed but to be envied."[2] We envy people for their success and esteem people for their character. Ours is a celebrity culture where success is measured by things like fame and popularity. Sadly, many Christian leaders also evaluate success by these measures. The failure to achieve success according to the values of this marketing-oriented society leaves many good people discontented.

I am puzzled by the fact some prominent Christian leaders, who seem to be very successful and attract large crowds to their programs, grossly violated biblical principles on their path to success. When discussing this problem, some have told me that sometimes people's gifts are not revoked even though God does not approve of their ministries (see Rom. 11:29). I am not fully convinced by this argument. One answer I have found to this problem is remembering

---

1 David E. Garland, *2 Corinthians*, The New American Commentary (Nashville: Holman Reference, 1999), 205.

2 "Artist Garry Trudeau, Creator of the 'Doonesbury' Comic Strip," *UPI* website, May 31, 1981, https://www.upi.com/.

that the church is a part of contemporary society. In society you can use methods not sanctioned in the Scriptures and still succeed. Good marketing and branding and skillful organization coupled with relevant meeting of felt needs can bring numerical success. If Christians use such methods, they too can succeed according to society's measures. But the fires of judgment will burn up these works like wood, hay, and straw (1 Cor. 3:12–15). At the judgment, the most important reckoning, these "successful" people will be found wanting.

Recently many famous people have crashed. The #MeToo movement revealed that many prominent people used their positions to sexually exploit others. This movement has come to the church also, and leaders are resigning from their posts at an alarming rate in the West. This is a problem in my part of the world also, and it will not be long before it comes to the surface here. Yet the crashes of many successful people have not been powerful enough to challenge the myth that selfish, unprincipled ambition is a noble and satisfying pursuit.

One of the greatest challenges that Christians encounter today is believing that it is worth following God's principles as taught in the Bible; it is truly worth paying the price of living according to one's principles. But we must persevere, believing that God will indeed honor those who honor him (1 Sam. 2:30). Would that Christ would say of us, as he said of Nathanael, "Behold, an Israelite indeed, in whom there is no deceit!" (John 1:47). The world desperately needs people like Barnabas, who was described as being "a good man" (Acts 11:24). Even though evidence might suggest otherwise, it is worth sticking to God's principles, if for no other reason than we can have the joy of knowing that God smiles upon us.

Refusing to Tamper with God's Word

The third thing that Paul refuses to do is "tamper with God's word" (2 Cor. 4:2). The word translated "tamper" appears only here in the New Testament. It is used in extrabiblical literature for the adulteration of wine. Paul is saying that he refuses to dilute his message by avoiding difficult topics and that he refuses to adulterate it by adding features that are incompatible with the gospel.

We have lived with ethnic tension in Sri Lanka for many decades. During our three-decade-long war, which ended in 2009, I sometimes felt it was necessary to speak about the issue of racial prejudice. People were often unhappy with what I said. I am told that I should not talk about difficult issues because they are too divisive. But if I am to be faithful to God's word, I must tell the people what the word says about hard topics. The same applies to issues like the absolute uniqueness of Christ. Many are diluting clear biblical teaching to fit into our inclusive, pluralistic culture. Of course, as Paul did in Athens, we need to find the best way to communicate our message (Acts 17:16–34). And, as Peter said, we must do so with "gentleness and respect" (1 Pet. 3:15).

Then there is the doctrine of judgment. It is a very prominent theme in the Bible. But it is not so in Christian preaching. Indeed, some have misused this doctrine and given it a bad name. But misuse should not result in disuse. We must creatively seek ways to persuade people of this key Christian doctrine.

What a challenge we have! The world's thinking on many issues is so different from the way we believers think. The answer is not to isolate ourselves from society and find refuge in our holy huddle. Indeed, we need like-minded friends who will encourage us to stay along the straight and narrow path, as we shall see later. But from the strength of such friendship we must go into the world and engage it with conviction, using the most relevant means available to argue for the truth of God's word.

Further Reflection

What challenges to your integrity come to you from the society and the Christian community to which you belong? What can you do to guard yourself from being contaminated by these dangerous influences?

13

Conscience: Others' and Ours

THE APOSTLE PAUL not only avoided things that compromised his integrity; he also aspired to something positive: ". . . by the open statement of the truth we would commend ourselves to everyone's conscience in the sight of God" (2 Cor. 4:2). Paul was being attacked by opponents for what he believed and who he claimed to be, but he did not dilute the truth or hide aspects of his message that were not palatable to others. Paul's response to attacks on his ministry was "the open statement of the truth."

Commend Yourself to the Conscience of Others

Paul knew that many would reject what he said. But he also knew that our choices and actions should not be controlled by those who criticize us. It is true that many will criticize, but others' consciences will agree with what we say. We hope that they will be encouraged by our message. What an important lesson this is! Because the ministry that many of us have is a public one, people are going to respond to it publicly. The response of some will be positive, and that of others will be negative. We listen to all the responses respectfully. But they do not ultimately determine how we choose to live.

When I give a talk, if ninety-nine people praise it and one person criticizes it, guess which response I will spend the rest of the day ruminating upon? The critical response! We all like to be appreciated. But that can be a dangerous motivation when considering what to speak about. Of course, we need to take criticisms seriously and learn from them. Many are valid. Some show that we have not accurately communicated what we intended to say. Others may show a flaw in our reasoning.

But ultimately what is important is what God thinks about what we say. So Paul says that he commends himself "in the sight of God." The final revelation of whether we did right or wrong will come only at the judgment. Believing this makes the blows we receive from people bearable. Later Paul says, "For this light momentary affliction is preparing for us an eternal weight of glory beyond all comparison" (2 Cor. 4:17). This is why we should always be thinking about the judgment. It gives us eternal perspective and helps shape our values.

This is one of the paradoxes of the Christian life. To some, judgment brings fear. But to us it is a source of comfort, an antidote to bitterness.[1] When people hurt us for doing or saying the right thing, we can be consumed by anger and bitterness. We who are committed to loving our enemies will surely be upset when they hurt us. But the discouragement does not overwhelm us. Actually, when we align ourselves with biblical attitudes, the anger is replaced by compassion. We reckon that if our enemy is doing something wrong, he or she will be judged for it. And that causes us to have compassion for the enemy.

1 I owe this insight to John Piper's book, *Future Grace* (Sisters, OR: Multnomah, 1995), 262–66.

We are also comforted from knowing that God sees and rewards the righteous. Hebrews 11:6 says, "And without faith it is impossible to please him, for whoever would draw near to God must believe that he exists and that he rewards those who seek him." A key to living the life of faith is believing that God rewards those who seek him, especially at the judgment. Without a firm grasp of the doctrine of judgment, we will be handicapped in the pursuit of a life that pleases God. A key motivation to costly obedience will be missing in our thinking. When the Salvation Army founder William Booth's son Bramwell showed him an article attacking him in the newspapers, he said, "Bramwell, fifty years hence it will matter very little indeed how these people treated us; it will matter a great deal how we dealt with the work of God."[2] Our job is to be faithful, anticipating the Lord's "well done."

But there is encouragement to the faithful in this life too. There is one more affirmation in 2 Corinthians 4:2 that we must look at. Paul says, ". . . by the open statement of the truth we would commend ourselves *to everyone's conscience* in the sight of God" (2 Cor. 4:2). There are sincere people who are committed to the truth, and they understand and approve of what we say. They encourage us along the path to faithfulness. They are not overly enamored by the world's values. They want to know whether what we say is true, and their consciences will guide them to accept the truth.

So we are encouraged by the opinion of godly people, and refuse to allow negative comments from others to detract us from the path of faithfulness. If our fulfillment comes from knowing that

2 Bramwell Booth, *Echoes and Memories* (London: Hodder and Stoughton, 1977), 8.

we have done what pleases God, then our joy is maintained, and a foundation is laid for maintaining freshness in ministry.

Take Pains to Have a Clear Conscience

This is a good place to discuss another conscience-related statement from Paul. When responding to charges made against him by the Jews before Governor Felix, Paul said, "I always take pains to have a clear conscience toward both God and man" (Acts 24:16). Though here Paul speaks of his own conscience specifically, he presents the general principle that doing what is right leads to freedom. The word translated "take pains" (*askeō*) means "to engage in some activity, with both continuity and effort—'to do one's best, to endeavor.' "[3] This is a serious pursuit. We are to be passionate about maintaining a clear conscience.

We have already looked at three reasons George Mueller gave for his long life. The third was the joy he felt in God and his work. The second was the refreshment he received from the Scriptures (see chap. 16). Mueller's first reason is pertinent to the present discussion. It was "the exercising of himself to have always a conscience void of offence both toward God and toward men."[4] It is a huge burden to go through life with unsettled spiritual business. The burden of guilt drains us of our energy and leaves us debilitated and devoid of the fullness of the Spirit. When we do not experience the peace of God, it can make us irritable and difficult to live with and work with.

Paul first told the governor Felix that he took pains to have a clear conscience toward God. Our constant exposure to sex, violence,

---

3   J. P. Louw & E. A. Nida, *Greek-English Lexicon of the New Testament: Based on Semantic Domains*, 2nd ed. (New York: United Bible Societies, 1996), 1:662.

4   *George Mueller: Man of Faith*, ed. A. Sims (Privately published in Singapore by Warren Myers), 51.

selfishness, prejudice, and dishonesty today have influenced us more than we like to acknowledge. Bad thoughts come to us all the time. We must quickly go to God without nurturing such thoughts and seek his forgiveness and cleansing. A few minutes before I wrote this, a pastor I mentor called me to say that he was being buffeted by bad thoughts. He wanted to unburden himself and free his mind by confessing this with me. In my prayer with him I thanked God for giving him a sensitive heart that desired to let the Holy Spirit always have full control over his thought life.

Next Paul said he took pains to have a clear conscience toward people. We must not let problems remain in our relationships with others without trying to resolve them. Sometimes when driving to preach I realize that there is something I need to clear up with someone, usually relating to something unwise or wrong that I said. When I don't have time to do that before I preach, I promise God that I will do it afterward.

When I was young, I was taught to keep "short accounts" with God and with others. If we have done something wrong, we must clear it as soon as possible before it can truly damage our relationship. John Bunyan (1628–1688) spoke of how some people "confess sins notionally and by halves." He said that is "dangerous because the wound is healed falsely."[5] We block grace through half-confessed sin. Often people confess only the part of their sin that was found out, and they hide the part that is not known by others. The price of half-confession is not worth paying. To lose grace is to lose our greatest treasure. We may avoid some temporary shame, but we forfeit the privilege of being people whom the Spirit can freely use, and we lose our greatest earthly wealth: the joy of the Lord.

5   John Bunyan, *Justification By an Imputed Righteousness*, in Roger C. Palms, comp., *Upon a Penny Loaf: The Wisdom of John Bunyan* (Minneapolis, MN: Bethany Fellowship, 1978), 18.

Let us take pains to have a clear conscience before God and people. That is a key to maintaining a constant supply of grace and preserving our freshness in ministry.

If we are to enjoy unhindered access to God's grace, we need the freedom of walking in the light with God and people (1 John 1:7). We must allow no incomplete transactions. Sins have been confessed and forgiven, and we are committed to fully following God's ways. From the world's viewpoint, this may be regarded as an unnecessary burden that hinders our standing and progress in society. But this is the only way to be free to minister with unhindered access to empowering grace. It may look like an unnecessary burden, but it is a key to persevering in ministry over the long haul with the freedom of knowing that God approves of our lives and service. Guilt is a debilitating burden to carry as we serve God.

Further Reflection

Can you think of any incomplete transactions with God or people that you need to settle in order to have a clear conscience? If you do have such, what will you do about it? If you don't have any, ask God to help you to continue living with no hindrances to his grace.

14

Contentment in a Celebrity Culture

THE AMBITION of any sincere servant of God is to glorify God through his or her life and ministry. Paul said, "So, whether you eat or drink, or whatever you do, do all to the glory of God" (1 Cor. 10:31). Our desire is to do well in ministry so that God is glorified. We want our work to be great so that people will see God's greatness, not to show off our talents or to be greater than others. But today we are hampered in this pursuit by false values, which present other kinds of ambitions.

False Understandings of Success

There is great freedom in being released from bondage to the world's standards of success. A sinful spirit of competition and envy and the desire to be better than others can deprive us of that freedom. In a media-saturated age with multiple competitions for measuring who is the "greatest" in numerous fields, it is easy to fall into the trap of measuring our significance using unbiblical criteria. We have lists of the greatest sportspersons, sexiest men and women, most popular or best actors and actresses, and so on. It's easy for those who don't make those lists to feel insignificant and inferior. Ours is a celebrity culture that measures significance based on things like fame, affluence, and the size of our work.

A false understanding of success is a major cause for many people feeling unfulfilled and unhappy as they serve God. I have seen books and heard talks that claim that everyone can be a leader if they follow the right prescription for leadership. If that were true, then those who are not leaders will be disappointed by their failure to achieve the "success" of being a leader. The biblical view is that leadership is a call, and those gifted with leadership ability will receive that call. One might say that only Peter, James, John, and Judas (for the wrong reasons) were famous out of the twelve apostles. But there is nothing in the Bible that says the others were not following God's will for their lives. Paul takes great pains to say that all Christians are equally significant whether their gifts give them prominence or not (1 Cor. 12:14–25).

Envy and a competitive spirit were problems among Jesus's disciples. Once they were arguing about who was the greatest, and Jesus's response was, "If anyone would be first, he must be last of all and servant of all" (Mark 9:35). I am convinced that most Christians who say they believe in the full authority of the Bible do not accept the authority of these words in their own lives. If for some reason they become "last," they get angry. For instance, what if someone else gets a promotion they think they deserve? Some let this anger fester inside of them until it ruins their joy and transforms them into people controlled by bitterness.

The disciples didn't immediately learn the lesson Jesus was trying to teach them. A little later, James and John asked for seats at the right and the left of Christ in the kingdom—a request that infuriated the other ten disciples (Mark 10:36–41). Again, this display of unbiblical ambition prompted some profound teaching by Jesus. He showed them that the world's method is to value those who have great authority over others (10:42). This is a measure of significance and success among Christians today too. We ask, "How many staff do you have working under you?" or "How large is your congregation?" But Jesus said, "It shall not be so among you" (10:43). Jesus's words here were similar to his earlier response: "Whoever would be great among you must be your servant, and whoever would be first among you must be slave of all" (Mark 10:43–44). Then he gives himself as an example as one who "came not to be served but to serve, and to give his life as a ransom for many" (Mark 10:45).

Even at the end of Jesus's ministry, the disciples struggled with this wrong understanding of greatness. Jesus demonstrated servant leadership by washing their feet and asked them to follow his example (John 13:3–17). But a little later we find them again disputing among themselves about who is the greatest (Luke 22:24).

I find the above sequence of events comforting. Even the disciples of Jesus found the biblical ideas of greatness and servanthood difficult to accept. We should not be overdiscouraged by our own failures and the failure of those to whom we minister to understand this truth. But like Jesus, we must consistently teach the same message and demonstrate its practical outworking through the example of our own lives.

The three words for envy and jealousy (*phthonos, zēlos,* and *zēloō*), which appear fifteen times in the New Testament, are things Christians must avoid. Envy is the result of thinking about significance using unbiblical categories. Jealousy also can ruin good people. It often makes them act like fools. When others sense that we are envious or jealous, they often don't alert us, thus adding to the shame.

In my younger years I served on the organizing teams of national and international conferences. The times of fellowship with

Christians of different backgrounds on those teams are some of happiest memories I have in ministry. But some of my unhappy memories involve our discussions of what public roles we should give to prominent people whom we hoped would attend the conference. Things like the following were said: "We'll have to give him a prominent role, otherwise he'll be upset. Let's give him a prayer at the opening ceremony!" The noble work of prayer had become a slave to the egos of insecure leaders.

What a contrast this was to the presence of John Stott at the Lausanne Younger Leaders Conference in Singapore in 1987. He was arguably the most prominent Bible expositor in the world at that time. And he came just to be an encouragement to us younger folk. He did not want to speak. We did have a question-and-answer session with him, and he graciously spent an hour of his time engaging with me personally.

Facing Rejection

If we are to experience ongoing freshness in ministry, we must fight to overcome the crippling effects of rejection. We must learn to accept disappointments without launching into a futile battle to restore our honor.

As stated earlier, many people who experience deep wounds before coming to Christ find acceptance within the Christian community. Some come to value the feeling of significance, perhaps too strongly. When they later experience what looks like rejection within the same community, it can be a painful blow. I have seen some such people overcome the pain of these blows through their passion for God, their passion for ministry, their earnest wrestling with God, and the patient encouragement of other Christians. But I have seen others destroyed by these experiences of rejection.

One of the saddest parts of my ministry is working with people who don't want to be healed from such wounds. They want to cling to the idea that they have been wronged. Hurt becomes a part of their identity. The sense that they have been wronged gives them an excuse for being angry. This leaves them vulnerable to making serious mistakes in life. If they encounter other experiences of rejection, they could overreact and become a spectacle, resulting in a severe loss of credibility.

Freedom from the Passion for Earthly Recognition

Once we are free from the need to showcase our abilities, to climb the ecclesiastical ladder, and to gain power and influence, we are also free to enjoy Jesus and the privilege of serving him. Our fulfillment comes not from our position in our church or organization but from the high privilege of serving our beloved Lord. New Testament scholar T. W. Manson has said, "In the kingdom of God, service is not a steppingstone to nobility. It *is* nobility, the only nobility which is recognized."[1]

If we relentlessly pursue earthly recognition, we can receive it by doing things appropriate for achieving that goal. But that does not automatically guarantee recognition by God. Three times in the Sermon on the Mount Jesus says of people who practiced religion for show, "Truly, I say to you, they have received their reward" (Matt. 6:2, 5, 16). The underlying idea behind this statement is that these people were fools for seeking earthly success. They have their reward, and nothing is left for eternity!

Sensitive servants of God learn to fear the trap of doing things for earthly recognition. Henry Clay Morrison (1857–1942) was

---

1 T. W. Manson, *The Church's Ministry* (Philadelphia: Westminster Press, 1948), 27.

the founder of Asbury Theological Seminary, where I studied. He was a great preacher and a brilliant orator. Once he was preaching at a camp meeting along with a younger preacher. One Sunday the younger preacher preached in the morning, and God's Spirit moved in the audience powerfully, resulting in many sinners seeking the Lord. When Dr. Morrison preached in the evening, the younger preacher was disappointed as he sensed that Dr. Morrison was trying to outdo him by using his great oratorical skills.

Later that night the younger preacher saw someone enter his tent. It was Dr. Morrison. "He stumbled around until he found the foot of his bed. He knelt at the foot of the preacher's bed, buried his face in the covers over his feet, and began to sob as if his heart would break." The younger preacher said nothing and let the transaction between Dr. Morrison and God continue. Many years later, that younger preacher, now an older man, told a young theological student, Dennis Kinlaw, "The Holy Spirit quickened [Morrison's] conscience and convicted him of the sin of it. He could not sleep until he had found his friend and acknowledged his sin." Kinlaw himself became a powerful preacher. After relating this story in his classic book, *The Mind of Christ*, Kinlaw says, "I'm glad Henry Clay Morrison had that kind of sensitivity to the Holy Spirit, because I found Christ as a result of the ministry of that man. My wife also found Christ under the ministry of Henry Clay Morrison."[2]

It is likely that we will all face the trap of seeking recognition or earthly power or authority. We may be full of ourselves but empty of the Holy Spirit. Speaking through the prophet Zechariah regarding the rebuilding of the temple, God told the governor, Zerubbabel, "Not by might, nor by power, but by my Spirit, says the LORD of

---

2   Related in Dennis F. Kinlaw, *The Mind of Christ* (Nappanee, IN: Evangel Publishing, 1998), 74.

hosts" (Zech. 4:6). When we speak or counsel or exercise discipline or sing or lead a meeting, we ought to have desperately prayed for God's help. We seek not for earthly recognition but for the fulfillment and guidance of God's Spirit.

Further Reflection

What challenges do you face from the false values of the prevailing celebrity culture? What do you need to do to remain contented amidst those challenges?

15

Innovation, Growth, Excellence, and God's Glory

SOME PEOPLE THINK that you cannot motivate people to produce high quality without competition. They point to the failure of socialist economies which sought to eliminate competition but ended up leaving people without a drive to do well. Indeed, competition may be successful in helping markets to operate, and it may be the law of the jungle. But it is not the method of the kingdom of God.

Many Christians think that competition provides a necessary motivation to nurturing effective ministries. As evidence they give examples of people who said that they were competing with no one, but they did not have success as an aim; rather, they said that their aim was to be faithful. But it was evident to all that they were ineffective in what they did. The noble idea of *faithfulness* has been discredited because that word has been used to describe "good" (as in harmless) people who have had mediocre ministries without innovation, growth, and excellence. They did not achieve much because they did not take risks or try new things. People say about them, "At least they were faithful."

Innovation and Strategic Thinking

But the Bible gives us a motivation stronger than competition when we desire innovation, growth, and excellence: God's glory. We have seen the glory of God and have been enraptured by it. We realize that we represent this glorious God on earth. Therefore, we wish for God to be glorified in all we do. As Paul said, "Whether you eat or drink, or whatever you do, do all to the glory of God" (1 Cor. 10:31).

So even though we do not compete with others or strive for recognition, we want to find the best way to do the work of God so that he would be glorified by it. This requires strategic thinking. The most innovative brains among God's people need to work to discover the best way to have the maximum impact for the kingdom of God. Paul was a master at this as he adapted his ministry style to be relevant and effective to different cultural audiences. He said, "For though I am free from all, I have made myself a servant to all, that I might win more of them" (1 Cor. 9:19). He went on to say that to win the Jews he became as a Jew; to win those under the law he became as one under the law; to win those outside the law he became as one outside the law; and to win the weak he became weak (9:20–22). He summarized his approach saying, "I have become all things to all people, that by all means I might save some" (9:22b).

Earlier Paul said, "For necessity is laid upon me. Woe to me if I do not preach the gospel!" (1 Cor. 9:16). Here was a man burning with a passion for the gospel. Because of his desire to make inroads for the gospel, he was innovative and thought strategically.

A study of his missionary methods shows his wise, bold, and innovative approaches to mission. Faithfulness for Paul involved strategic thinking.[1]

I led the work of Youth for Christ in Sri Lanka for thirty-five years. Our mission is to reach young people who would not come in contact with the gospel through usual channels. Strategy is therefore very important to us, and our strategies change as cultures change from place to place and from era to era. But I am not a gifted strategist. I was primarily a Bible teacher and shepherd to our staff. So I had to depend on others to do the strategizing, and I would try to help create an environment where they felt free to try out their creative ideas. If we do not have the gift of strategic thinking, then we must rely on others to do that. Passion for the gospel pushes us to strategize.

We don't compete with others to have the biggest church or ministry. But passion for the glory of God makes us concerned with numbers because numbers represent lost people who have been saved. The book of Acts makes eleven references to the numbers of those who are saved (2:41, 47; 4:4; 5:14; 6:1, 7; 11:21, 24; 14:1; 17:4, 12). We desire to grow not for the sake of growing, but so that we can have maximum impact on the lives of people in need of Christ.

Excellence

Just as passion for the glory of God makes us committed to strategic thinking and to bringing the gospel to as many people as we can, it also makes us committed to excellence in all we do. We want to reflect

---

1 See Roland Allen, *Missionary Methods: St. Paul's or Ours?* (Grand Rapids, MI: Eerdmans, 1962); Dean S. Gilliland, *Pauline Theology and Mission Practice* (Eugene, OR: Wipf and Stock, 1996); and Eckhard J. Schnabel, *Paul the Missionary: Realities, Strategies and Methods* (Downers Grove, IL: InterVarsity Press, 2008).

the glory of God in the way we do our ministry and in all fields: music, counseling, preaching, teaching, evangelism, administration, and more. It is a tragedy when God is not glorified through our programs. Sometimes people see the quality of our programs and feel sorry for God because his representatives are so incompetent. They have been responsible for a great tragedy: the dishonoring of God.

Sometimes those who strive for excellence in public ministry can neglect excellence in personal work. We must avoid that trap. Public ministry arises out of personal ministry. Those who are not conscientiously ministering to individuals will lack depth and penetrative insight in their public ministries. The key to excellence in personal ministry is working with individuals with patience and perseverance despite their many weaknesses.

Those who are not committed to excellence in what they do for God will soon lose their freshness. A driving ambition to do what they do well is replaced by an addiction to mediocrity. They soon get bored, and service becomes an unexciting routine. And their attitude can influence the mood of their whole team.

As with innovation and growth, a passion for God's glory drives us to excellence. Johann Sebastian Bach (1685–1750) has been described as "in many ways the father of Western classical music."[2] When he completed a piece of music, he would write at the bottom of the page the letters *SDG*, for *Soli Deo Gloria*: "To the Glory of God Alone." Because Bach's ambition was to glorify God, he needed God's help. So before writing a piece he often wrote at the top of the page the letters *JJ* for *Jesu juva*: "Jesus help."[3]

2 "Why Is Bach So Great?," Astraios Chamber Music website, August 20, 2018, https://www .astraiosmusic.org/.

3 "The Life and Faith of Johann Sebastian Bach: 'Soli Deo Gloria' (To the Glory of God Alone)," Christianity.com, December 9, 2022, https://www.christianity.com/.

This passion can be a source of freshness in our lives. It gives us a holy ambition, which drives us in our work and drives away boredom. Now we do not compete with others, but we compete with ourselves. It makes me want to be the best Ajith Fernando that I can be—all so God may be glorified through the quality of my work.

Handling Mixed Motives

But it is easy for this push for growth and excellence to become selfish ambition. As long as we are on earth, we will struggle with mixed motives: the desire for self-glory mixed with the desire to bring glory to God. Of course, when we are praised for what we have done, it is right for us to be happy. We live and work to bring honor to God, and when people are blessed by what we do, we can rejoice that our goal has been achieved. We don't need to deprive people of the joy of expressing their appreciation by rebuking them and saying, "Give glory to God alone." But the prospect of praise should never influence our decisions to do what we do. Sometimes we must do or say something that people will not like. Out of our commitment to the glory of God, we will do it and face the criticism that may come.

So we persevere, aware that our motives may be mixed. We keep asking God to purify our motives, remembering that God "knows our frame; he remembers that we are dust" (Ps. 103:14). Ultimately what is important is not our performance but God's work in and through us, his unworthy servants. When our loving Father sees our work influenced too much by the self, he will send a discipline to get us back to the perspective of living for his glory alone. As Hebrews 12:6 puts it, "For the Lord disciplines the one he loves, and chastises every son whom he receives." The verb translated "disciplines" (*paideuō*) means to "instruct, train, teach, discipline."[4] From that word we get the English word *pedagogue*, which means teacher.[5]

God's discipline may be painful to bear (Heb. 12:11). It may even be humiliating to us. I believe that seemingly small, inconsequential things can be acts of disciple from the Lord. A microphone causes a loud squeak while we are singing a solo. An open-air rally for which we laboriously prepared is ruined by a storm. A slip of the tongue while speaking elicits laughter from our hearers. Of course, if some human negligence has caused the disruption, then we should address it so that it doesn't happen again. But generally, when something humiliating happens due to no fault of our own, we can say to God, "Thanks, I needed that."

Albert Orsborn (1886–1967) was a songwriter and general of the Salvation Army. When he was a young officer in London, revival spread in the area where he had been leading. Following this revival another officer told him that he heard that the leaders were planning to divide his district. He urged Orsborn not to let it happen. He said that God was blessing his district so much and that dividing the district would hinder the work of God. He told him, "I think you ought to fight it." Orsborn replied, "Oh, no. I want to do the will of God and respect my superiors. I will not do that."[6]

But he did begin to argue with the leadership. Later he said that the real reason for his arguing was because his prestige and power were reduced. "Unwittingly I had begun to fight not for the

---

4 Barclay Newman, *Greek-English Dictionary of the New Testament* (New York: United Bible Societies, 1971).

5 Bruce M. Metzger, *Lexical Aids for Students of New Testament Greek* (Grand Rapids, MI: Baker Academic, 1998), 34.

6 I first shared this story in my *Deuteronomy: Loving Obedience to a Loving God* (Wheaton, IL: Crossway, 2012), 639–40, after reading it in Dennis F. Kinlaw's *The Mind of Christ* (Nappanee, IN: Francis Asbury Press, 1998), 72–73.

kingdom but for my position in the kingdom, and the Holy Spirit was grieved." He said, "When the Spirit grieves, the Spirit leaves."[7] He said he went through the motions of ministry, but there was a distance between him and God. Deadness had entered his life, and he felt empty inside.

Then Orsborn had a car crash, and he took a long time to recover. God began to work on him. One day he heard some singing in the room next to his in the hospital. He said, "I heard them sing of the glories of God. My heart began to yearn once again for that kind of intimacy with God. I wept my heart out in repentance. God forgave me. And the Spirit came and filled my heart afresh."[8] Thank God, Orsborn went on to have a powerful ministry and ended his life well.

After I have completed writing a book, I often find myself failing in the very area about which I have written. Upon completing my book *Reclaiming Friendship* (Herald Press, 1993), I had serious problems with a friendship. After writing *Jesus Driven Ministry* (Crossway, 2002),I experienced some major failures in my ministry. After finishing *The Call to Joy and Pain* (Crossway, 2007), I felt deep discouragement that challenged the joy I had written about. I have come to see these as warnings from God not to think of myself as an expert. I am forced to acknowledge that I am a learner in the school of Christ, struggling to serve him with a pure heart.

As believers, we each have made a commitment to be totally committed to God and serve him for his glory alone. Every day that commitment will be challenged. Much of the challenge will have to do with the quest for earthly significance: our position, exercising

7   Kinlaw, *Mind of Christ*, 72–73.
8   Kinlaw, *Mind of Christ*, 72–73.

authority, our privileges, and adequately using our gifts. May we battle these temptations and thank God when he disciplines us in order to purify our motives.

Further Reflection

What areas in your life and ministry need to be more innovative, in order to experience growth and exhibit the excellence that befits God's glory? Are there some steps you need to take to progress in these areas?

16

Refreshment through Our Call and the Scriptures

A KEY TO MAINTAINING FRESHNESS in ministry is having a sense that what we are doing is significant. Our calling and gifts should never be our primary source of fulfillment and security. That place belongs to God. But knowing that what we are doing is meaningful and eternally significant becomes a reason for contentment and thus joy in our lives. Whether we are in vocational ministry or are serving the Lord as volunteers, all Christians have the assurance that they have been equipped with gifts to fulfill a role that is of eternal significance in God's kingdom. Can there be anything more significant than that?

The Joy of Being Called

The joy of being called and equipped with grace is expressed in Paul's autobiographical account in 1 Timothy 1:12–17. He thanks God for appointing him to his service (1:12) and then reflects on the grace that lies behind his salvation and call (1:13–17). He mentions that even though he was a blasphemer, "the grace of our Lord over-flowed" for him (1:13–14). This causes him to reflect on the gospel which lies behind his salvation: "The saying is trustworthy and deserving of full acceptance, that Christ Jesus came into the world to save sinners, of whom I am the foremost" (1:15). Then he says that his own conversion was an example of how God has patience with those who believe (1:16). Paul then bursts into a powerful doxology: "To the King of the ages, immortal, invisible, the only God, be honor and glory forever and ever. Amen" (1 Tim. 1:17).

The above is my favorite passage in the Bible. It presents the sheer thrill of knowing that, though we are undeserving people, God has saved us and given us an amazing work to do: to be his ambassadors on earth (2 Cor. 5:20). As a child I struggled with a strong sense of inferiority, which caused me to be very shy and quiet in public. I often felt discouraged and would get upset about myself. Then, at the age of fourteen, I became a committed Christian through the influence of my family, especially my mother.

Soon I began to feel that God was calling me to be a preacher. But I dared not tell anyone about it. I guess I thought that people might laugh at the idea that a person who was scared to open his mouth in public wanted to be a preacher. I had a friend who lived in a region where there was no church nearby, so by the age of about seventeen I began writing a sermon every week and mailing it to him. I lived near the sea. The desire to preach became so great that I would go to the beach at night and preach to the rocks on the seashore. Soon I became involved in our church youth fellowship and in Youth for Christ. I began to get opportunities to speak, and people recognized that I was gifted in that area. I was gripped by a passion for the work of God. I realized that I could not afford to waste time feeling sorry for myself. There was work to do!

As a teenager I knew that I was a child of God. But that head knowledge had not traveled to my heart. I still struggled with a strong sense of inferiority. The fact that God had given me a work to do helped that truth to make the journey from the head to the heart. Later I learned that I should not rely on ministry to be my primary source of identity and significance. God—and my relationship with him—was my source. But the sense that God had given me a job to do helped affirm my significance and made me believe in my heart that I was indeed his valued child. The excitement about being God's servant still remains with me almost six decades later. And the memory of my struggle with inferiority has become a trigger for immense joy over my identity in Christ and call to be his servant.

Freshness through the Word

Not only is our call a source of joy, but the material we work with, the Bible, is also an excitingly rich resource bringing freshness to our lives. It is the Creator's unique word to his creation. It is powerful to bring about change in people. It is "living and abiding" and able to bring people to be "born again" (1 Pet. 1:23). It cuts through people's defenses and shows them who they really are. Hebrews 4:12 says, "The word of God is living and active, sharper than any two-edged sword, piercing to the division of soul and of spirit, of joints and of marrow, and discerning the thoughts and intentions of the heart." And it helps effect genuine change in a person's character (Ps. 119:9, 11; John 17:17).

The Bible is not only the book we preach from; it is also the book we live by. The psalmists mention thirteen times that they delight in the word (Pss. 1:2; 111:2; 112:1; 119:14, 16,

24, 35, 47, 70, 77, 92, 143, 174). Using the language of passion, the Psalms say that God's word is desirable because it is sweeter than honey (Pss. 19:10; 119:103). This is the material with which the Christian communicator works. Rodney "Gipsy" Smith (1860–1947) was a British evangelist who preached the gospel for seventy years. He died of a heart attack at sea on his way to the United States at the age of eighty-seven. When asked the secret of his freshness and vigor, he responded, "Sir, I have never lost the wonder of it all."[1]

One of the sad consequences of all the technical aids to sermon preparation that are available today is that they can deprive us of the thrill of grappling with God's word. An extreme example of this is generative AI models, such as ChatGPT, which can generate sermons based on texts or subjects tailored to specific audiences. Indeed, such aids can save us a lot of time and give us some helpful information. But among the many limitations of relying solely on technology is that we miss the thrill of wrestling with the word. Handling the word during preparation to teach and preach has a way of feeding our souls.

As for me, I have lived with a fairly rigorous schedule in my forty-seven years of ministry. But I have always found myself refreshed as a result of giving extended time, amidst my busy schedule, to grapple with the truth of God's word. Sometimes I go to prepare a message feeling discouraged and tired, but the time spent in preparation actually energizes me afresh.

Jeremiah, suffering from the public humiliation of punishment by the chief officer of the temple, considered giving up his work as a prophet. But he could not. He said,

---

1   "Hymn History: I Have Never Lost the Wonder of It All," Enjoying the Journey website, https://enjoyingthejourney.org/. Accessed July 11, 2022.

If I say, 'I will not mention him,
> or speak any more in his name,'
there is in my heart as it were a burning fire
> shut up in my bones,
and I am weary with holding it in,
> and I cannot. (Jer. 20:9)

He was compelled by the powerful message God gave him. His mood was not one of happiness. But he was compelled by the Holy Spirit. I would call that freshness in ministry!

At one point Jeremiah was deeply discouraged by the seeming fruitlessness of his ministry and the sense of being forsaken by God. But in the middle of a lament expressing his gloom, he recalled the sweetness of the word that had gripped him at the time of his call:

Your words were found, and I ate them,
> and your words became to me a joy
> and the delight of my heart. (Jer. 15:16)

The psalmist said, "If your law had not been my delight, I would have perished in my affliction" (Ps. 119:92).

The second reason George Mueller gave for his long life of ministry was the love he felt for the Scriptures and the constant recuperative power they exercised upon his being.[2] Bruised and battered by the blows we receive from ministry, we come to the Scriptures and are confronted by "the living and abiding word of God" (1 Pet. 1:23). Our insecurity is attacked as we sense the reality that "the world is passing away along with its desires, but whoever

---

2 *George Mueller: Man of Faith*, ed. A. Sims (Privately published in Singapore by Warren Myers), 51. For the other two reasons, see chapter five.

does the will of God abides forever" (1 John 2:17). Freshness returns despite the gloom that surrounds us.

May we go to the Scriptures daily with the anticipation of the psalmist who prayed, "Open my eyes, that I may behold wondrous things out of your law" (Ps. 119:18). Of course, we do not find emotionally uplifting passages every day. Some passages, especially in the Old Testament, may sound quite boring. But when we spend time even with such passages, we buttress the idea that we are grounded in something that is sure and from our eternal God.

The year 1989 was a dark year in my country's history. A revolution occurred, led mainly by a group of young people. Tens of thousands of youth died, some of whom I knew and had talked to about Christ. I was often engulfed by a sense of gloom. My wife and I had decided that whatever happened outside, we would keep a happy home for our children. But my moods were not helping. One day my wife told the children (so that I could hear!), "Father is in a bad mood. Let's hope he goes and reads his Bible!" She embraced a rich theological truth. Despite the terrible things that are going on in the temporal world, we can maintain our peace if we are rooted in the eternal world of which the Bible speaks.

The psalmist said, "Great peace have those who love your law; nothing can make them stumble" (Ps. 119:165). That is security!

Freshness through Scripture-Based Books

The security that comes from the Scriptures is further enhanced by reading Scripture-based books.[3] When we do this, we are enjoying material related to the source of our security. This affirms our call when our pragmatic society keeps feeding us material that suggests

---

3   Some points in this section are from my book, *Jesus Driven Ministry* (Wheaton, IL: Crossway, 2003), 104.

that what we are doing is a waste of time. We need to conscientiously battle the trend to find satisfaction in reading and watching readily available but shallow entertainment in the media. We must look for material that gives us lasting enrichment. Though some of that can be found on the internet through high quality podcasts, blogs, and periodicals, the value of print books is that we can read them slowly, taking notes as we go along. Unlike listening to a talk, we can stop to reread, think, and pray.

When I was a student at Asbury Seminary, missionary scholar Bishop Stephen Neill spent a few days at the school. I tried to take advantage of every opportunity to listen to him. Once a student asked him a question about reading, and I have tried to follow what Neill said in his answer for almost fifty years. He suggested that we go through a serious theological book slowly for however long it might take, reading a little at a time. For me these reading adventures take several months per book. But they have greatly enriched me and shaped my thinking.

I heard about a minister who left the ministry and went into other work because he was burned out and discouraged. He even left his personal collection of books behind in his last church. His successor found that most of the ex-pastor's earlier books were on the Bible and theology, while most of the books he had acquired more recently were on practical topics. He was a typical product of our pragmatic age. Certainly books on practical matters can be helpful supplements to a robust biblical and theological library. But pragmatism alone will not help us to remain fresh in ministry over a long period.

The Uniqueness of Our Message

Related to the thrill of handling the word of God is the realization that we have been called to be the ones who proclaim God's unique word to the world. We are the ambassadors of the King of kings (2 Cor. 5:20). And this work is powerful in effecting change. God changes lives through preaching. Paul argues, "How then will they call on him in whom they have not believed? And how are they to believe in him of whom they have never heard? And how are they to hear without someone preaching?" (Rom 10:14). Later Paul said, "How beautiful are the feet of those who preach the good news!" (10:15). I tell our young staff in Youth for Christ that most photographs don't give the real picture of our beauty because they do not generally show our beautiful feet!

Robert Murray M'Cheyne (1813–1843) was a Scottish preacher who lived only thirty years but had a huge impact for the kingdom. He quoted someone he calls Henry as saying, "I would beg six days, to be allowed to preach the seventh."[4] I once heard Dr. Michael Raiter, the former principal of the Melbourne School of Theology, describe a conversation he had with an elderly Australian preacher. Raiter asked him, "Do you ever feel like giving up?" The preacher answered, "No." Raiter asked him how that was possible. He said, "I think of the angels. The angels in heaven can do many wonderful things. But there's one thing they cannot do. They can't preach. And that I can do."

Handling Scripture and realizing the glory of our call energizes us. Braced by the conviction that God still uses preaching to effect change in people's lives, we persevere in our call. One of the sad results of the postmodern downplaying of the value of objective truth has been a downplaying of the value of words as a means of communicating truth. But disdain for what we preach is not something new. Even Paul said, "For since, in the wisdom of God,

4   Robert Murray M'Cheyne, *A Basket of Fragments* (Inverness: Christian Focus, 1979), 8.

the world did not know God through wisdom, it pleased God through the folly of what we preach to save those who believe" (1 Cor. 1:21). So we persevere in seeking to find the most faithful and creative ways to present the unchanging truth of the word.

The Trustworthiness of Scripture

Before I close this chapter, I need to say that in some circles it has become fashionable to doubt the trustworthiness of the Scriptures. Some of the blessings of refreshment that come from handling God's word are lost when we doubt the reliability of what the Scriptures say. I have seen preachers who used to preach from the word with much power and conviction lose that power after they went for higher studies and lost their belief in the trustworthiness of the Scriptures. They remained good people whose character was a challenge to me, but their preaching had lost its power.

Servants of God need to grapple with the question of the reliability of the Scriptures until we come through with a firm conviction about the word. Famous Christians like Billy Graham and G. Campbell Morgan experienced a crisis of belief that led to a strong, affirming belief in the trustworthiness of the Scriptures, which was a key to their effectiveness in ministry.[5]

I was exposed to a lot of liberal preaching in my youth. Some of these preachers lived exemplary lives that challenged me. I studied theology in the United States at a time when the so-called "battle for the Bible" was raging. Esteemed scholars were questioning the inerrancy of the Bible. During my first Christmas vacation in the States, I read the book *Fundamentalism and the Word of God* by J. I. Packer.[6] It helped me understand that there is a good case for

---

5 For more on Graham's and Morgan's experiences, see *Jesus Driven Ministry*, 128.

6 J. I. Packer, *Fundamentalism and the Word of God* (Grand Rapids, MI: Eerdmans, 1958).

believing that the Scriptures are trustworthy. That belief has been battered by many questions over the years, some of which I have not resolved and have held in abeyance awaiting further knowledge. But I am able to preach the word out of the conviction that "all Scripture is breathed out by God and profitable for teaching, for reproof, for correction, and for training in righteousness, that the man of God may be complete, equipped for every good work" (2 Tim. 3:16–17). Because it is inspired by God, the Bible is powerful in effecting change in people's lives.

With such conviction, we can proclaim God's word with confidence and be refreshed as we handle Scripture to prepare to use it in ministry. We have a great call, and we have a great book to equip us to fulfill that call!

Further Reflection

Do the Scriptures and the call of God upon you renew you as described in this chapter? Do you need to make some changes in your attitude for that to happen?

17

Grace through Friends

FROM MY PERSONAL EXPERIENCE and my observation of others I can say that a major reason why many servants of God do not maintain freshness in life and ministry is that they are not able to handle their weaknesses well. They make mistakes or poor choices; or their weaknesses become sins; or their brilliant projects flounder because of a lack of administrative oversight. These issues become huge burdens that sap their energies and ruin their credibility. Again, from my own experience and through observing others, I can confidently say that many of these problems can be avoided if we have friends who walk alongside us, who know us and our weaknesses, who encourage us when we are down, and who have the freedom to speak into our lives with rebuke and advice. Friends are a key to maintaining freshness.

The description of a seminar on "Why Christian Leaders Need More Friends" begins with these words: "The research is startling: friendship has been proven to boost our health, decrease anxiety and depression, increase our lifespan, and be a buffer against addictions, prejudice and extremism. And yet rates of it are declining in the

West."[1] This is a problem all over the world. Over thirty years ago, seeing an acute need for the recovery of biblical friendship, I wrote *Reclaiming Friendship*.[2] I have been advocating for the formation of friendships among Christian workers in Sri Lanka ever since. Unfortunately, I cannot say that I have been very successful outside my own ministry circles.

I do not know where I would be if not for the friends I have had over these years of ministry. They have been God's agents of healing, encouragement, direction, and accountability in my life. I will always be enthusiastic about the blessings of friendship. And when I say "friends," I include mentors, spouses, those whom we disciple, siblings, and even our children.

The Jesus Model

In his final discourse before he died, Jesus told his disciples, "No longer do I call you servants, for the servant does not know what his master is doing; but I have called you friends, for all that I have heard from my Father I have made known to you" (John 15:15). Jesus spent a lot of time with his disciples, discipling and teaching them.[3] Those whom we disciple, mentor, or supervise could, through unhurried time spent together, become our dear friends, just as the disciples became friends of Jesus.

Much of the teaching in the Gospels emerged from situations the disciples encountered when they were with Jesus and the questions they asked him along the way. These "holy conversations" helped

---

1   Sheridan Voysey, "Why Christian Leaders Need More Friends," Forum of Christian Leaders website, May 22, 2022, https://foclonline.org/.

2   Ajith Fernando, *Reclaiming Friendship* (Leicester, UK: Inter-Varsity Press, 1991; Scottdale, PA: Herald Press, 1993).

3   For more on this, see my *Discipling in a Multicultural World* (Wheaton, IL: Crossway, 2019). See chapter 8, "Learning the Truth."

them understand the mind of Christ. Jesus would often hide away from the crowds so that he could spend time with his disciples. Our relationships with our friends may differ from Christ's relationship with his disciples, but the idea of "holy conversation" must surely be a part of any good friendship. Chatting about the things of the Lord or about the things of this earth from a Christian perspective helps knit hearts together. Christians delight in the truth, as the Psalms often remind us. Talking about such delightful subjects is one of the richest blessings of friendship. We all need a circle of like-minded people whom we enjoy.

Many people have told me that it's hard for them to have close friends because it is difficult to trust others. They have been hurt by friends who betrayed confidence. But one of the results of meeting with like-minded people for extended periods is mutual trust. This does not guarantee that there will never be betrayal. But it reduces the chances of that happening. We do not like to hurt those for whom we have developed an affection.

But making time for such extended conversations takes commitment. Our orientation toward constant activity can cause us to almost unconsciously allow programs to crowd out time for meeting with friends. Long conversations are countercultural in a world that communicates through short messages and sound bites. It requires a firm commitment to schedule such meetings. Sometimes, meeting electronically through video platforms can help. That is how I survived the COVID pandemic lockdown periods in 2020–2022. But face-to-face physical meetings are even more enriching. My experience is that a group of friends, like an accountability group, requires one person to take the responsibility of organizing in-person get-togethers. Otherwise, they are too easy to overlook.

The Bible talks about many other blessings of friendship. We will focus on four of them from Ecclesiastes 4:9–12 in the next two chapters.

A More Fruitful Life

Ecclesiastes 4:9 says, "Two are better than one, because they have a good reward for their toil" (Eccles. 4:9). Friends help us to succeed in life. For those in ministry, friends help us to be more fruitful in our work.

My first paid job was as National Director of Youth for Christ, Sri Lanka. I had been a full-time student until I was twenty-seven years old, and I was thrust into the leadership of a growing organization. My colleagues on staff knew more about ministry than I did. I realized that if I were going to succeed as a leader, I would have to depend on my colleagues. And they were amazing! They helped me with difficult decisions. They were much more visionary in their outlook than I was, and that helped the movement move into creative new ventures. They helped me avoid naive mistakes coming from inexperience. On my part, I tried to care for them, teach them the word, keep the vision of the movement burning, and give them the space and encouragement to try out new ideas. I was forced into the conviction that effective Christian ministry is team ministry.

Let me mention two specific blessings that come from friends to help us to be more effective servants of God. Our friends' *prayers for us* have a powerful influence in our lives. Paul described Epaphras as "wrestling in prayer" for the church from which he hailed in Colossae (Col. 4:12 NIV). Paul knew the power of prayer and depended on the prayers of others to be conduits of grace in his ministry. He said, "You also must help us by prayer, so that many will give thanks on our behalf for the blessing granted us through the prayers of many" (2 Cor. 1:11; see Eph. 6:18–19, Phil. 1:19).

About five years ago I had a lovely experience of such prayer while I was on a sabbatical in the States. A young staffer I was mentoring was under attack in a WhatsApp group. He had made a mistake in a claim he made for our ministry, and when others found out it was untrue, a few began to punch him with verbal blows. I was halfway around the globe praying for him during this time. Each time he was given a blow, I gave a counter prayer-punch on his behalf. It was a beautiful experience of friendship over the miles.

Of course, we must realize that when we ask for prayer, we make ourselves vulnerable to misunderstanding. Some people will give us advice or criticism, which we may consider unfair. People may scold us for doing something they believe was foolish. But these friends will pray. And that makes the criticism worthwhile. Everyone in ministry needs to cultivate an army of people who back them in prayer. That takes commitment. We must faithfully present our needs and also faithfully report on how the thing they prayed for turned out. Some will not find the time to read and pray; that's inevitable in our information-overloaded world. But some will pray, and those friends are a great treasure.

Our friends can also give us *wisdom for making decisions*. Many respected servants of God have made foolish decisions, especially toward the end of their ministries. Some have launched into projects aimed at leaving a legacy behind. These projects often become white elephants after they die. But because they were respected servants of God with a long and distinguished record of service, others don't want to express their reservations about the projects. After they die, maintaining the projects become major burdens. Whether we are junior or senior in ministry, we can be blinded to pitfalls related to our ideas because of our emotional tie to the idea. Therefore, it is always safe to have others who help us with decisions, especially relating to ministry projects and finances.

When I served on the Lausanne Committee for World Evangelization over three decades ago, the committee always seemed to be short of funds. At that time, Billy Graham was the honorary chairman of the committee. He was the most prominent Protestant leader in the world at that time, and his organization had the ability to raise a lot of funds. We thought that they could help us. But when the topic was brought up, people close to Graham said that although he would like to help us, his board would not let him. Here was the most prominent leader at that time; funds came in because of his name. But he chose to be subject to a board when spending these funds.

Proverbs 12:15 says, "The way of a fool is right in his own eyes, but a wise man listens to advice." The need for wisdom from friends applies in many other areas too: in the choice of a life partner, when making decisions about our personal finances, before making a major investment in things like a house or a vehicle, and when making choices regarding career changes. Our friends can see things that we do not see because of our enthusiasm for or emotional tie to the idea. They can help us avoid making big mistakes.

Of course, our friends are not God. They can make mistakes too. We are enriched by friends but not enslaved to their opinions. God may give us a vision that seems too radical to others. At such times, without angrily discarding our friends and going it alone, we must prayerfully and humbly persevere until God opens the door to fulfilling our vision. Sometimes that door may lead us to a structure separate from the one to which we have belonged. But that separation must be handled lovingly and patiently in a way that honors Christ.

Over the years I have spent a major portion of my time studying, and perhaps I have accumulated a considerable amount of knowledge. But I know that I often lack the wisdom needed to apply this knowledge to difficult situations. I am so grateful to my wife and my friends who have guided me at such times. They have helped me avoid making serious mistakes. C. S. Lewis has written a lot about friendship and how much he owes to his friends. He wrote, "The next best thing to being wise oneself is to live in a circle of those who are."[4]

Early in his Christian walk John Wesley went to see someone he described as "a serious man" who told him, "Sir, you wish to serve God and go to heaven. Remember you cannot serve him alone; you must therefore find companions or make them; the Bible knows nothing of solitary religion."[5] We need to "find" friends, but that is a difficult task. Often our quest ends in disappointment. If we cannot find them, we must "make" them: patiently nurture friendships that will become deep and trusting enough to enable us to share on a deep, personal level.

Further Reflection

Do you have a few people you can call your close friends, as described in this chapter? What obstacles do you need to overcome in order to forge such friendships?

---

4   C. S. Lewis, *Selected Literary Essays*, "Hamlet: The Prince or the Poem" (1942). Cited in Wayne Martindale and Jerry Root, *The Quotable Lewis* (Wheaton, IL: Tyndale, 1989), 233.

5   John Fletcher Hurst, *John Wesley the Methodist: A Plain Account of His Life and Work* (New York: Eaton & Mains, 1903), 64–65.

18

Friends in Times of Need

THE LAST CHAPTER showed how friends can help us to be more effective in life and ministry. But perhaps the greatest blessing that comes from friends is their help when we are in trouble. How often we hear people say that there was no one in the church to help them in their time of serious need. When we hear such comments, we need to seriously ask whether we care for people inadequately. But sometimes people received no help in times of need because they had not cultivated deep friendships before they faced the problems.

When Jesus faced the greatest challenge of his life in Gethsemane, he did so in the company of his close friends Peter, James, and John (Mark 14:33). Following the first incident of public opposition to the gospel, when Peter and John were told for the first time that they were not allowed to preach the gospel, they immediately "went to their friends and reported what the chief priests and the elders had said to them" (Acts 4:23). The word translated "friends" is used for people with whom one has a close relationship. They had a close group to go to.

Ecclesiastes 4:10–12 presents three ways friends help us when we are in need.

Lifting Us Up When We Fall

Ecclesiastes 4:10 says, "For if they fall, one will lift up his fellow. But woe to him who is alone when he falls and has not another to lift him up!" We can fall in different ways. We might fail in an enterprise or project; we might lose an election; or we might fall into sin. Our reactions to a fall can be erratic. We might become overdiscouraged. We might stop battling temptation and go deeper into sin. We might make foolish decisions in response to the situation. Let's focus here on help we receive after we have succumbed to temptation.

The Greek verbs *homologeō* and *exomologeō* are usually translated "confess" and take a variety of meanings. Five times they are used with the idea of confessing sins (1 John 1:9; Matt. 3:6; Mark 1:5; Acts 19:18; James 5:16). In each of those times the confession is done within the context of the community. Indeed, we confess primarily to God. But, like many of God's blessings to us, healing from sin is often mediated through the help of others in the body. James says, "Therefore, confess your sins to one another and pray for one another, that you may be healed. The prayer of a righteous person has great power as it is working" (5:16). The healing referred to here may be physical healing or "restored spiritual well-being due to confession and forgiveness"[1] or both.[2] Whatever the exact meaning, it is clear that confession within the community is used

---

1 Craig Blomberg and Mariam Kamell, *James*, Zondervan Exegetical Commentary on the New Testament (Grand Rapids, MI: Zondervan, 2008), 245.
2 Douglas J. Moo, *The Letter of James*, The Pillar New Testament Commentary (Grand Rapids, MI: Eerdmans: Apollos, 2000), 245.

as a means of recovery from sin. Sharing with others relieves a huge burden that we have been carrying alone. It also helps us take constructive steps along the path to recovery.

Confession also helps us to get off of a dangerous path after we have erred. Early confession helps prevent major scandals. Often before a scandalous fall, one has made smaller follies. If nipped in the bud, the process leading to the major fall might have been averted. For example, a man and a woman might be doing ministry together on the same team. They understand each other very well and enjoy spending time together. They have a comradeship as brother and sister in Christ. But both might be unaware that the relationship is slowly moving in an intimate direction. Because it started so well, they don't realize what is happening. Others, however, see it, and it is their responsibility to warn them. If others choose to say nothing, a major scandal might occur.

I have had three occasions when I sensed that something bad might be happening with three sets of people in ministry. I saw that the way they were relating to each other was not normal. But I did not know them well enough to ask them about it. All three ended as major scandals, which ruined the ministries of good servants of Christ. True friends will be faithful in sensitively, graciously, and humbly confronting people when they see alarming behavior. A bad friend will gossip to other people about their suspicions. And a fool will refuse to take the warnings of faithful friends seriously.

Often our sins reveal our weaknesses; and though there is forgiveness for sin, we probably require healing from weaknesses. For this, discipline may be necessary. It is unfortunate that, though discipline for children is generally accepted in Christian circles, it is enacted with Christian adults only when there is an exceptionally grievous sin like fraud or adultery. Hebrews 12 has much to say about discipline in the life of a Christian. For example, " 'The Lord disciplines the one he loves, and chastises every son whom he receives.' . . . For what son is there whom his father does not discipline?" (Heb. 12:6–7).

Discipline can be painful. But the pain is part of the process of healing the weakness. Hebrews says further, "For the moment all discipline seems painful rather than pleasant, but later it yields the peaceful fruit of righteousness to those who have been trained by it" (Heb. 12:11). The word translated "discipline" here is *paideia*. From that word we get the English word *pedagogue*, which means teacher.[3] The word translated "trained" is *gymnazō*, from which we get the word *gymnasium*. Both of these words point to discipline being a training process. Indeed, it is painful, but the memory of the pain helps us avoid a recurrence of the sinful act.

I have made up the following story to illustrate this. Imagine that an excellent worship leader has a problem: she loses her temper with her husband and uses insulting language when scolding him. Her close friends know about this, because she shares her failures with them. Finally, the friends tell her that if she speaks to her husband that way again, she will need to stop leading worship for a period of three months. It does happen again, and she submits to the discipline. Sadly, the person who takes her place is not gifted in leading music. The person under discipline suffers during the three months that the interim leader leads worship.

She happily returns to her role after three months. One day her husband does something that makes her quite upset. As before, nasty words well up within her. But before they leave her mouth, she remembers her three months of suffering. She cuts off the unkind

---

3 Bruce M. Metzger, *Lexical Aids for Students of New Testament Greek* (Grand Rapids, MI: Baker Academic, 1998), 34.

language that nearly spilled out of her mouth. The discipline acted as a preventative to her falling again.

Discipline is not punishment; it is medicine for healing. Of course, it also demonstrates the holiness of a God who does not tolerate sin in the life of a believer.

Can We Trust Friends with Our Secrets?

Unless the whole church is affected by a major sin, we should keep people's problems confidential. Talking about genuine love, Peter said, "Above all, keep loving one another earnestly, since love covers a multitude of sins" (1 Pet. 4:8). When our friends talk about their sins, the first thought that should come to us is, "How can I help this person recover?" Or to use the language of Ecclesiastes, "How can I lift him up?" We look at sin from the perspective of grace knowing that "where sin increased, grace abounded all the more" (Rom. 5:20). When our passion is restoration of the person, we will not support anything that might hinder restoration. Gossiping about it therefore is out of the question.

Discipline works in communities of grace. I have been told more than once that one reason why pastors don't talk about their problems with each other is that there is a spirit of competition among them. One wants to be better than the other. It is not safe to talk about our weaknesses among our rivals. But in a grace-filled community everyone is acutely aware of their unworthiness. They rejoice in the fact that God has had compassion on them despite their unworthiness. They are painfully aware of how they fall short of an adequate response to grace. But they are also joyously aware that the merciful God forgives them when they do wrong.

In such grace-filled communities the passion of the members is to be holy, and they know they are not so. So they will join with others who are on a similar quest. Their passion for holiness makes them follow the exhortation of Hebrew 10:24: "And let us consider how to stir up one another to love and good works." I fear that, apart from being unable to trust people to keep confidences, there is another reason why at least some don't develop relationships of spiritual accountability: they are lacking in a passion for holiness.

A vision of abounding grace and a passion for holiness make people seek out spiritual comradeship that includes confession. How sad it is that many servants of God who have become entangled in sin had no loving community to help them before it got out of hand! How sad it is that many Christians did not have a community that could help them recover after they had committed a sin.

Emotional Support

Ecclesiastes 4:11 says, "Again, if two lie together, they keep warm, but how can one keep warm alone?" This imagery is drawn from the Middle East, where it can be very warm during the day and very cold at night. Travelers cannot carry heavy blankets with them. But if they sleep next to each other with their outer cloaks over them, they can keep warm. In the same way our friends can give us emotional support when we face the cold, harsh realities of life in an insensitive and sometimes hostile world.

We all face disappointment and rejection in our lives and ministries. At such times we need friends to whom we can go for understanding, guidance, comfort, and strength. But that takes commitment. In a busy, efficiency-oriented world, where convenience is a high value, only truly committed friends will give the unhurried time needed to adequately support us at such times.

Sadly, not many are willing make such a commitment to friendship. We are in an era of disposable relationships when "unfriending" is simply a matter of clicking a screen. People drop relationships when they become inconvenient. The words of Proverbs 18:24 address this well: "A man of many companions may come to ruin, but there is a friend who sticks closer than a brother."

Paul had a huge crisis, which he describes in 2 Corinthians 1. But he reports about this as one who has been comforted by God. We must wait until chapter 7 to see how that comfort came to him. He first describes the turmoil within him: "For even when we came into Macedonia, our bodies had no rest, but we were afflicted at every turn—fighting without and fear within" (2 Cor. 7:5). Then he writes that his mood changed: "But God, who comforts the downcast, comforted us by the coming of Titus" (2 Cor. 7:6). The comfort of his friend Titus took away the bitterness of Paul's pain. Later from prison he tells the Colossians about a few Jewish believers that "have been a comfort to me" (Col. 4:11).

Some of the greatest pain in life comes to us from people. And God often uses people to heal our pain through the comfort they bring. You cannot be angry with the human race when there are some humans who genuinely care for you. To be sure, our most reliable source of comfort is God. David said, "For my father and my mother have forsaken me, but the LORD will take me in" (Ps. 27:10). But when some people forsake us, God often sends others, like Titus, to mediate his comfort.

Some pastors and Christian workers today are angry at the way they have been treated by the church, by those they served, and by others. They have been faithful in their service to the kingdom, but in their later years they are not joyful over their experience in ministry. Some are bitter, others are disappointed. The freshness is gone. Good friends could have helped them overcome their bitterness and let the joy of the Lord permeate their lives.

Help in the Battles of Life

We all face battles in our personal and ministry lives. How we respond to them is key to our long-term effectiveness in ministry. Our passage in Ecclesiastes says that friends are a key to living healthy lives despite the battles we face: "And though a man might prevail against one who is alone, two will withstand him—a threefold cord is not quickly broken" (Eccles. 4:12). Over the past few decades, we have lived through wars and revolutions in my country. The presence of the military on our roads is a common sight. But we almost never see a soldier on duty alone. Though we have inspiring stories of individual war heroes and their exploits, the normal way of battling in a war is as a team.

I want to look at two kinds of battles servants of Christ encounter. The first is *our battle with our personal weaknesses.* Under this we can include such weaknesses as gossip, a quick temper, lust, lack of planning and self-discipline, stubbornness, and wasting time online and in front of the TV. Let me discuss the last of those challenges.

We are called to minister in a sinful world. Even though we may not participate in certain sins, we need to know about them, and the media is one of our sources of information. Unfortunately, spending time with various media, especially the internet, can give us a kind of pleasure that can become addictive. Our brains respond in a way that makes the pleasure addictive.[4] I am not referring only to pornography. We waste time on seemingly harmless things like stories on YouTube and pursuing gossipy news items.

4   See Brad Huddleston, *Digital Cocaine: A Journey Toward iBalance* (Vereeniging, Republic of South Africa: Christian Art Publishers, 2016).

Soon we can find ourselves close to addiction to these means of "relaxation and information."

One way to battle this is to find "safe" sources of information. I find the regular bulletins sent out by *Christianity Today* and the Gospel Coalition very helpful as well as articles in respected newspapers and periodicals. I once found a popular source of Christian news that focused so much on scandal within the Christian community that I began to feel impure through the exposure. I unsubscribed.

Another way to battle this is spiritual accountability with friends. Once the habit of too much exposure to the media has formed within us, our personal, private commitment to stay away and control our watching is not enough. Our friends can be an invaluable resource here. Christians believe that God is everywhere. That alone should prevent us from visiting bad websites, but it doesn't. But if a friend walks into the room while we are watching something we shouldn't be watching, we immediately click off that page. We seem to be more afraid to sin in front of our friends than in front of God!

Knowing that we are susceptible to temptation, God gave us friends to help us in our pursuit of holiness. Paul said, "Flee youthful passions and pursue righteousness, faith, love, and peace, *along with those who call on the Lord from a pure heart*" (2 Tim. 2:22). A key then is to find sincere Christians (those with a "pure heart") who will help us to flee from wrong passions and pursue holiness. I have two friends along with my wife who receive reports of my internet watching. One gets a weekly report from the software app Covenant Eyes. But that does not monitor time wasted or forays into gossipy news. So I give them a verbal report. And if necessary, a discipline is enacted.

Proverbs 27:5–6 says,

> Better is open rebuke
>> than hidden love.
> Faithful are the wounds of a friend;
>> profuse are the kisses of an enemy.

We all need faithful friends who love us enough to wound us and help us along the path to holiness.

I will only briefly discuss another battle we often face in ministry: *the battle with those who oppose us.* Many fine servants of God have lost their credibility and influence because of unwise responses to attacks or criticisms they have encountered. They act on impulse, and often that action is a foolish one. They might send a letter of resignation or take a personal matter that could have been settled personally out into the open for everyone to see. I have learned never to respond to an attack without getting advice from trusted friends. Very often my initially planned response has been vetoed by these friends. Most often my friends point out that, though I meant one thing, what would have been communicated was something very different (see Prov. 12:15).

Nurturing trustworthy, committed friendships could spell the difference between success and failure in life and ministry.

Further Reflection

What safeguards do you have to help you in your battle for a holy life? Can you add more benefits from close friends to your list?

Conclusion

IN CHAPTER 2, I gave the sad statistic that in the Bible and in the church today it seems that only about one-third of Christian leaders end their careers in service well. But I also said with emphasis: *It does not have to be so!* In this book I have attempted to substantiate that statement by showing how we can serve God over the long haul with freshness and joyful contentment.

My main contention has been that God's grace is sufficient for every challenge and that he is able to give us freshness that can help us face every challenge that comes our way.

- We are joyful about being loved and saved by God. As his beloved children, we have been given gifts that enable us to do significant work for the kingdom. The knowledge of this identity and significance helps attack the insecurity that causes many unhealthy attitudes and behaviors.
- God's joy-giving presence sustains and empowers us amidst our weakness and comforts us when we face difficult experiences so that we do not need to live with bitterness over our circumstances.
- God gives us friends and colleagues who provide companionship that attacks the loneliness that is the lot of many

of God's servants. These friends comfort us, encourage us, and correct us when start down harmful paths.

We have also considered things that can hinder God's free flow of grace to our lives and have a debilitating effect on our freshness, including the following.

- Acting against our consciences and not settling sin issues through repentance and forgiveness.
- Not setting aside time to be with God in prayer and the Bible.
- Succumbing to unbelief, which gives us a wrong attitude toward the problems we face.
- Quitting, rather than groaning with God, when things go wrong.
- Lacking a commitment to excellence and innovation, which results in lethargy and monotony in our lives and ministry.
- Embracing wrong ambitions, which owe their origin to our sinful selfishness and the false values of our celebrity-oriented society.

As you seek to maintain freshness in your own life and ministry, let me encourage you with two quotes from Paul that have ministered to me greatly over the years:

And I am sure of this, that he who began a good work in you will bring it to completion at the day of Jesus Christ. (Phil. 1:6)

He who calls you is faithful; he will surely do it. (1 Thess. 5:24)

General Index

Scripture Index

Also Available from Ajith Fernando

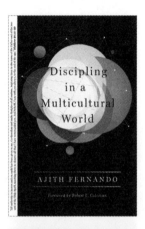

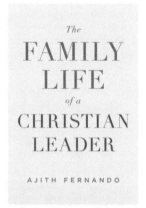

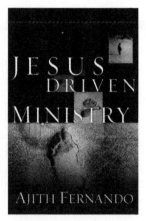

For more information, visit **crossway.org**.